E

MW00615525

This book is filled with stories from a 20-year career of caring for some of the most needy of the planet's peoples, and in some of the most challenging and difficult places—Burkina Faso and Madagascar. Santmyire's passion is, through these stories, to encourage and equip others to take up the challenge of caring in a world that shows little interest in caring for other human beings. Drawn in his youth to serve others in Africa, he chose nursing as a career that would equip him for this passion and give him essential skills to meet very basic human needs. The journey of serving has enriched his life in far more profound ways, as he listened, learned, adapted, and served people with vastly different afflictions, fears, personalities, expectations, and cultural experience. This book reflects deeply upon that journey, bringing readers into the real worlds of suffering people, learning how to communicate with and care for them, and to lead others to join him in the "art of caring" that reaches beyond the limits of technology and science. If you have the slightest inclination to join him in this journey, you will be enriched by his insights, challenged by his questions, and better equipped for the uncertainties of a life more complex than you ever imagined.

Sherwood Lingenfelter, PhD
Senior Professor of Anthropology
School of Mission and Theology
Fuller Theological Seminary
Pasadena, CA

In a day where caring for each other has become less common, Aaron has written a book that challenges and equips each of us to be more intentional about how we care. He uses his own life story and his adventures in Africa to illustrate and encourage each of us to consider how we can each have *A Caring Life.*

Donna L. Barrett
General Secretary
Assemblies of God USA
Springfield, MO

If you want a powerful intellectual, emotional, and cultural journey with the Spirit at every turn, *A Caring Life* is the book for you. Aaron's range of experience and research is rich and refreshing. He and his family have lived what he writes. When he states early on that "dignity is the impetus for caring," I knew I wanted to hear what else he had to say. I was challenged to my toes. Enough said. I'm buying a case!

Dick Foth
Author, A Trip Around the Sun *(Batterson and Foth), and* Known: Finding Deep Friendships in a Shallow World *(Dick and Ruth Foth)*

In the glorious work of making disciples and planting churches among unreached peoples, we have seen over and again that love, truth, and power entwine. The insertion point is arbitrary. Sometimes you begin with declaring God's truth from God's word. Sometimes the journey is started because of God's power manifested in healing, deliverance, miracle, or a dream. And sometimes it is love that opens the door of the heart. All are necessary and all are present in God's mission to rescue and restore men and women to Himself from everywhere and all peoples. In this excellent book, *A Caring Life*, Aaron skillfully shows us how to love and how to care daily, so that it is who we are, not merely what we do.

Dick Brogden
Co-Founder
Live Dead Movement
Jeddah, Saudi Arabia

At a time when love and care for each other seems at an all-time low, Aaron brings us practical and timely insights and actions steps to live out Jesus' command to love one another. Although I wish we didn't need it, we can all use this handbook on caring. May we learn to be better at giving care, and better at receiving it. Thank you for the gift of this book, Aaron.

Kadi Cole
Leadership consultant and executive coach
Author, Developing Female Leaders

Aaron's book, *A Caring Life*, touches more than emotions; it also reaches into our cognitive processes and deep into our souls. The book is appropriately titled, yet I feel it is even more a record of growth along a journey of caring. I recommend it for anyone on this same journey—one modeled by Jesus—a life of caring for others.

Greg Mundis, D.Min.
Executive Director
Assemblies of God World Missions
Springfield, MO

A Caring Life is a beautifully written book concerning the importance of, the heartbeat behind, and the nuances of providing care for others. It's jam-packed with Aaron's personal stories, hard-hitting quotes, and practical insight on how we all can become better caregivers to those around us. What I love most about this book is its uncanny way of making me examine my own life and commitment to give others the Christ-like care they deserve. It's my belief that anyone that dares to care well will thoroughly enjoy this much needed resource.

Cornell A. Jordan
Pastor, Metro Assembly of God
Youngstown, OH

In today's climate, the exhortation from James that "faith without works is dead" is more relevant than ever. The work that James references is caring with action. *A Caring Life* brings to the forefront how to care with deeds that focus on those requiring care. This care is central to the gospel we bring.

Arnold Bracy
Care Pastor, Cornerstone Church
Bowie, MD

During the pandemic, the need for belonging and the importance of caring for our neighbor surfaced in tangible ways for many people. However, many people felt ill-equipped to care for the hurting in their communities. Aaron invites the reader on a journey to explore how we can show up for one another and communicate care and belonging in meaningful expressions.

This book will change your perspective and methodology for caring, if you're open to change.

Shannon Polk, D.Min., JD
President and CEO
Ann Arbor Area Community Foundation
Ann Arbor, MI

Most people know that caring for others is important. However, the demands and distractions of life so often keep that knowledge from translating into thoughtful action. In *A Caring Life*, Aaron Santmyire provides an inspiring call to embrace the art of caring in everyday life. His adventure-filled stories combined with practical application ideas are inspiring and convicting. He brings powerful perspective on a practice we often take for granted, and his depth of insight is challenging and refreshing. No matter what stage of life you're in, this book will stretch you and equip you to care authentically, love unconditionally, and lead compassionately.

Stephen Blandino
Lead Pastor, 7 City Church
Fort Worth, Texas
Author, Stop Chasing Easy

It has been my honor and joy to lead and work with Aaron for almost two decades. Aaron has spent his missionary life caring for and loving people. He has established care pathways for the missionaries of Africa AGWM. For many years, in Madagascar, Aaron focused on developing innovative ways to reach, engage, and care for some of the world's most needy people. Aaron's capacity to be Jesus' hands and heart extended to the people he serves is huge. He lives a life of care and service and has reproduced the same many times over in people he has trained.

Greg Beggs
Regional Director
Assemblies of God World Missions Africa
Springfield, MO

As leaders who care for a fellowship of churches and ministers, we have transitioned to a relational network where caring is at the forefront. Aaron's statement of "with leadership comes authority and great responsibility, and if organizational culture is not caring, the leader holds the responsibility to change it" speaks volumes, and we are listening. *A Caring Life* is a must-read book for all, especially for leaders seeking cultural change.

Frank Potter
Superintendent of Potomac Ministry Network of the
Assemblies of God

Lisa Potter
Author, The Collective Journey, *and Executive Director*
of Women Who Lead

A

How Each of Us Can Change the

CARING

Trajectory of an Uncaring World

LIFE

Dr. Aaron Santmyire

ISBN-13: 978-0-578-29822-1

Printed in the United States of America.

To Heather, Isabelle, and Josiah:

*You have taught me more about
a caring life than anyone else.*

*Thanks for loving me when I am
Aaron and when I am Ron.*

Table of Contents

Foreword

Living in our world is not easy, and some days it can seem to get more difficult by the hour. From overwhelming anxiety caused by a global pandemic to the increasing fears of present and future conflicts in our world, life today can be a bit much, to say the least. On top of these public fears are the private struggles and personal pains that people face each day. Millions of people are walking around with severe hurt and intense stress that can be physically debilitating, and all too often they go unnoticed and uncared for. It's ironic, isn't it, that although humanity has billions of devices that allow us instantaneous connectivity to anyone anywhere in the world, we are less caring as a society now more than at any time in history.

Living out a *caring life* does not happen on a whim. It is a choice. It is not based on simple emotion or a momentary response. It is a decision to be someone who cares deeply about what people are walking through; to be someone willing to walk alongside hurting people and offer emotional, tangible, and long-term commitment; and to be someone who comes alongside another to bring hope and wholeness. A *caring life* requires much more than simply liking a post or sending that quick heart-emoji response. It is caring at a level that goes well beyond your comfort level. It is a level of care for hurting and hopeless people.

It has been my joy to walk with Aaron for many years, to watch him live out a *caring life* wherever he has lived. From his small-town roots in West Virginia to the villages and over-crowded cities of Africa, from those suffering with HIV/AIDS to a homeless person, Aaron consistently conveys a deep, personal desire to care for others—not just when it's easy, but even when it's hard. It has been an honor to walk with Aaron as a friend, partner in ministry, and mentor.

In the pages that follow, Aaron writes what he is living out, not as a theorist but as a practitioner. You will hear his heart on each page, and you will discover that a life of caring is some-thing we are all called to do. I know you will be challenged by the great stories and great truths, and you will learn how to give care at all times by all means. Accept the challenge that Aaron puts forth to make a *caring life* more than a phrase, but to make it a lifestyle lived out that can change a hurting world one life at a time.

Mark Lehmann
Lead Pastor
Cornerstone Church
Bowie, Maryland

Preface

The year 2020 was a season of personal frustration, disillusionment, and discontent. I knew God called me to care for others in Africa, but doubt and second guessing began to take over a large portion of my mental space.

Questions rhythmically rattled through my heart and mind: What have I spent the last 20 years of my life doing? Has it been worth it? What impact have I made? Have I been a wise steward? Do I really want to do this for the next 20 years?

Maybe you have asked yourself similar questions during a season of contemplation. I called it my "journey of rediscovery," but those closest to me, my wife included, called it my "midlife crisis."

Either way, during this time of deep spiritual reflection in which I examined the past, considered the present, dreamed about the future, and asked others to speak into my life, I was also reading the book *Convergence* by Brett Johnson in which he writes about everyone's natural talents, acquired abilities, and spiritual giftings. I pondered this idea of Convergence, asked others what they saw in my life, and prayed that God would reveal what He was doing in my life. As I did, a tapestry, woven in the past with a common uniting thread, slowly unfolded in the present.

The thread was a *caring life.*

My venture into a *caring life* began when I enrolled in Allegany Community College (ACC) in Cumberland, Maryland, to pursue an associate degree in nursing. I had applied to several different schools but ultimately chose ACC because it was a family tradition (my mom, aunts, and cousin had graduated from the same nursing school), and it had a great reputation for preparing students to pass the required state board certification exam to become a registered nurse. The college also happened to be near the grand, bustling metropolis of Wiley Ford, West Virginia, my hometown.

Incidentally, I had no great desire to be a registered nurse. My 18-year-old self was not overly excited about male nurse jokes, though I had thick enough skin to ignore them. Nor was I looking forward to the questions about not becoming a doctor. I truly considered becoming a doctor until I learned about the amount of school debt one racks up. I knew being a medical doctor was not for me as such debt would delay my plan or hinder it entirely because what I knew from age 12 was that I was called to live and serve in Africa, and I was convinced that nursing was my ticket to remaining debt-free so that nothing would slow my pursuit of the dream God placed in my heart. Nursing was how I would pay for my next degree and it would give me a portable skill to use around the world.

But nursing, the profession I entered hesitantly and without the best motives, impacted my life in a profound way. In fact, on day one of nursing school I was presented with the concepts and framework that became the focus of the rest of my life. I remember sitting in class listening to my professor Dr. Susie Tasker Weaver discuss the syllabus and its *exciting* content (a little sarcasm here), wondering when she would get to the good stuff: all the anatomy, physiology, microbiology, immunology, and everything else that intrigued and challenged me. I wanted her to jump right into all the topics that excited me. Instead, she began by talking about the ethos of nursing and nursing theories. Admittedly, I was about as excited about the ethos of nursing and nursing theory as I was about the syllabus, but I was interested in passing the class, so I dutifully sat at my desk and took notes. I am so thankful I did because the concepts my professor shared that day still rumble through my mind 20-plus years later.

I remember my professor said that the heart or ethos of nursing was caring, and I remember thinking, "Caring? I signed up for caring? I thought I signed up to be a nurse and make money. I came to learn about injections, anatomy, pharmacology, all the interesting things, not about a profession based on caring."

At the heart of nursing, she said, was caring for a person as they walked through the disease process, that nurses do not treat a sickness. She shared that at its very essence, nursing focuses on caring for the person and on the importance of listening, learning, and building trust with the person so you can care for them. In her experience, it was challenging, at best, to care for someone who did not trust you. She challenged us to not focus on just the disease or sickness and not to let anatomy and physiology take priority. She said that the *whole* person who was facing the disease, sickness, or life challenge was of utmost importance. The *whole* person was at the forefront of the why of what nurses do what they do. She further delineated how nursing focuses on caring and is complementary to other medical professions as they focus on curing.

That day in nursing school in Cumberland, Maryland, I signed up to be a nurse, and that meant learning to listen, observe, and learn from and about people so I could care for them. In one way or another, that is what I have been doing ever since.

In my journey of rediscovery, I was reminded that I worked on my master's degree in nursing while in language school in France so I could better care for and serve others when I moved to Africa. I recalled that when my family moved to Burkina Faso, I was the only man serving in a clinic that cared for women infected with HIV/AIDS. We provided medication and formula for women and their newborns so that the newborns did not contract HIV/AIDS. I also remembered that my wife Heather and I served with a colleague in a support group that cared for those living with the reality of having HIV/AIDS in a world so often unkind to those struggling with it.

I thought about how more recently my focus in caring for people extended to dermatology, thanks in large part to the training I received from my sister Beth who is a doctor. To some, given all the challenges in Africa, skincare does not seem that important, but my sister taught me that by caring for someone with a skin condition, we can have a dramatic impact on their emotional, psychological, and physical health. I have noticed as I have cared for people that whether poor or rich, male or female, educated or uneducated, regardless of race or ethnicity, the majority of people care about first impressions and how others see their skin.

I remembered how this concern for how others see our skin was evident to me while caring in Madagascar. I traveled to rural and remote areas caring for a broad range of skin diseases with a specific passion for caring for those with *chromoblastomycosis* and leprosy. Both of these diseases dramatically impact the lives of those afflicted with them, and many times those suffering from these diseases are ostracized and stigmatized be-

6

cause of the strong smell coming from their rotting skin or from the fear others have of contracting these diseases.

Considering my life over the last 20 years in France, Burkina Faso, and Madagascar, the common uniting thread that emerged in the tapestry was caring. Caring was the natural talent, acquired ability, and spiritual gifting with which God had entrusted me.

Caring is not always convenient, easy, fun, or even safe, but I have learned that caring is vitally important and desperately needed. No matter where you are in the world, there will be people all around you who need care, and that is why I am sharing my thread of a *caring life* with you.

Why This Book Now?

O ver the last 20 years as I have traveled and lived in countries like France, Burkina Faso, Madagascar, and Kenya, I
have observed that caring for the people that cross our paths
has become more and more uncommon. Whether the people are
family, neighbors, colleagues, employees, classmates, athletic
teammates, or the restaurant server, it is my perception that our
society is becoming less interested in caring for each other, and
at times, not even concerned about caring for oneself.

Perhaps it's the endless monologues on social media instead
of healthy dialogues, the drift towards isolation rather than
community connection, or the shift towards individualism over
the greater good. Or maybe it's due to the complexities and effort it takes to truly care for someone. I do not know all of the
reasons and how they interplay, but the reality is Jesus called us
to love and care for each other, and I just don't know how well
we're doing.

In preparation for this book, I did several searches for books
on the idea of caring. There are books about the care of pets,
the care of a lawn, and the care of an elderly parent. But what
about the care we have the opportunity to provide others each

and every day? Unfortunately, there were few books on caring for humans. The list of opportunities to care for others is long: caring for someone who has received an unexpected diagnosis or has been laid off or has lost a child or has a son or daughter who has chosen a different path in life and so on.

So, then I asked myself, "What are some of the reasons caring is becoming less and less common in our world?" The complexity of caring may be one reason we are shying away from it.

I recently read a book in which the author wrote about moving away from complexity. After World War II and the dropping of the atomic bomb on Nagasaki, the scientists and physicists struggled with their role and what they had done in developing the atomic bomb that took so many lives. Albert Einstein, although opposed to the bombing, had in some ways triggered the development of the bomb when he warned President Roosevelt of the real possibility of the Nazis developing their own weapon. In 1946, at the Princeton Conference, Einstein was asked about humanity's inability to control its new technology. The reporter specifically asked, "Why is it that when the mind of man has stretched so far as to discover the structure of an atom, we have been unable to develop the political means to keep the atom from destroying us?" Einstein replied, "That is simple; politics is more difficult than physics."[1]

Technology today continues to develop all around us, but we have fallen way behind in how we care for each other. We have made great advances in time management, vision casting, marketing, strategic engagement, and organizational and business growth. We have created things that simplify our lives and give us more time, but we fail to use that time to care for those who are more meaningful than what we created.

Borrowing from Einstein, perhaps caring, like politics, is more complicated than nuclear physics, and we simply do not know where to begin.

Something has to change. If our caring does not change, our family members, team members, neighbors, employees, and others around us will feel more and more like commodities than individuals with great dignity. They will see themselves as a mere cog in the wheel of our lives rather than someone of great value. So, the choice is ours: to engage more intentionally in the complexities of caring *or* to continue down the path we are on. One of my main goals with this book is to give you tools and skills that will help unravel some of the complexities of caring and help you develop a game plan to navigate them.

What to Expect

The chapters ahead include vital concepts about caring that I believe can help us turn the tide. We will explore the art of caring and the reasons it truly is an art. We will look at common barriers that hinder us from caring. We will discuss the importance of communication, that you communicate care in a way that is clearly understood. We will also talk about clarifying expectations and assumptions in caring, motivations in caring, caring when you are weary, your source for caring, caring when you are criticized, and caring cross-culturally.

Please hear my heart in this. I am not saying that I have this all figured out, that I am the authority or guru of caring, or that my thoughts are the right and only way. My hope is that this book will inspire and provoke conversations about a topic that is vital for teams, communities, families, businesses, and organizations today. I pray that you use this book and its concepts as a "campfire" to sit around and share openly, honestly, and transparently with a group of trusted family or friends.

Caring: A Working Definition

Before jumping into why caring is vital for the world today, it is paramount to consider what caring means in the context of this book—humans caring for humans. I wholeheartedly acknowledge that we can care for animals, plants, or other living things. The focus of this book is caring for human beings. I also recognize there are many different definitions and perspectives presented by theorists and caregivers on what caring is and how it is demonstrated. The definition I have chosen to use for the purpose of this book is: *Caring is the culturally appropriate actions that communicate dignity and value and that the receiver interprets as demonstrating that they belong, matter, and are known. In short, caring is the actions that meet the needs of belonging, mattering, and being known.*

A few important things to remember as you dive into the book:

1. This book is written for anyone who desires to grow in caring for others. Caring is not just for professionals. If so, we are in trouble. There are too many people in the world. If we leave caring to the professionals only, there is no way the tide will turn.

2. The stories I included are there for a reason. I recently shared a message at a local church in the States and someone approached me after and said that they rarely remember anything about a message other than the stories. For a speaker or teacher, this is humbling. But with that in mind, I use sto-

ries and life experiences here to highlight or further solidify the concepts I'm sharing. The stories do have a purpose, and that's why they are included.

3. As you read, you may quickly come to realize that I am a follower of Jesus. I am that unashamedly. How I care for people is deeply and richly shaped by His teachings and His commandments. You may not agree with me; I realize that. Please know that this book is not just for those who share my belief in Jesus. I care for and have dedicated my life to caring for people whether they believe the way I do or not. I care for people because I believe each person has inherent value and dignity.

4. Consider laying aside the "Hitler scenarios" as you read. In my mind, Hitler scenarios are extreme cases. Do not let them hijack the essence of the book. If such a scenario comes to mind as you read, such as an abusive, unsafe person, someone who could hurt you emotionally, physically, or in any other way, I recognize the concepts in this book do not apply. I consider those the outliers (five percent or less of people). This book is meant to speak to the other 95 percent of people, and not these outlier cases.

5. I am a learner and researcher at heart. I listen to 20–25 podcasts a week and read at least five or six books a month. It gets murky at times as I try to determine what are my original thoughts and what are thoughts I have learned from others. I have done my best to cite authors and sources throughout the book. If there are ideas or thoughts with missing citations, it is not intentional or me claiming someone else's work as my own.

6. This book is written in chapter format that will afford you the opportunity to process the concepts and topics by yourself or with others. Each chapter ends with a section entitled "Developing Your Caring Life." In these sections are practical questions that I have crafted to help you take steps on your caring journey. These questions take the concepts in this book and help you think, pray, and process so that you can grow your *caring life*.

Well, as I say in the introduction of my podcast, "there is no better time than now to get started, so here we go!"

CHAPTER 1

Why Care?

I n Morgantown, West Virginia, was a small house on a major thoroughfare that led to West Virginia University (WVU). Living in that house, in the shadow of that university, were seven children who watched dapperly dressed young people walk to and from class every day, young people who looked like they were having the time of their lives as they pursued this coming-of-age experience.

But it was an experience none of the seven would ever have on offer, as the situation life handed them made it impossible to receive an invitation. They held onto hope for a better life. But attending the university they could see and hear was as out of reach as having an elephant transport them around town.

It was the mid-1920s and the family was in dire straits. The father left his wife and seven children for reasons that only he understood. He left them with little money, little food, and little time. The rent on their house on the thoroughfare was paid until the end of the month, but after that they would need to find another place to live.

As it happened, the end of the month came, and the family was forced out of the home. The mother worked as hard as she could, but it was impossible for her to keep up with the rent and food for her seven children. So, they moved into an apple orchard. Yes, an apple orchard. The owner of the orchard offered them a place to stay under the trees and allowed them to eat any of the apples that fell to the ground. The family used the apples to supplement the little amount of food they had.

Fall is a beautiful time in the West Virginia mountains as the leaves begin to change, but for this family, fall and colorful leaves brought shorter days and colder nights. The only way to stay warm was a fire, and the only firewood they had was their possessions. They burned their possessions one by one in an attempt to stay warm. To say times were desperate is an understatement. First, they burned the larger wooden items, though they did not have many. As they burned through their bed and dresser, the family knew they would soon need to burn more precious things if something didn't change. Things didn't change and some of the last things they burned were the baby dolls of the younger girls. For a family that had experienced so much heartache and pain, the burning of the baby dolls was demoralizing and discouraging, and the pain of that memory was palpable for years to come.

Finally, the oldest sister had enough of the burning of their possessions to stay warm, eating just enough to get by, and sleeping out in the cold. While in town one day, she saw a sign at a church that advertised a harvest time picnic. The sign said it was open to anyone, which seemed too good to be true. She gathered the courage and asked the pastor if she could come. He responded kindly and welcomed her to the morning church service and then to the picnic.

She went home so excited about the opportunity for a free meal. She shared the great news with the rest of her family, but no one else was nearly as excited as she was. No one was interested in a church service even if there was a picnic afterward. They thought they simply did not fit in.

But the oldest sister was undeterred, and on Sunday she made her way to the morning service and the picnic, and then returned to the church for the evening service. At church, she was once again confronted with the fact that life was throwing more at her than she could handle: Her dad had left and was not coming back; she lived and slept outdoors in an apple orchard and burned things to stay warm; and every day she watched students all around her have fun (as they should) and dream of a bright future (as they should). She needed help. She needed someone to care for her. As the oldest, she did a lot of caring for others, but she needed to be cared for herself.

That Sunday at church, she got a lot more than a picnic lunch. She was cared for. She was fed both spiritually and physically. She made a commitment to turn her life over to Jesus. Her smile, which had long since disappeared, returned. The pastor and the church rallied around the family and cared for them at the lowest point of their lives, and in doing so, set into motion a series of events that not only changed the present situation but impacted generations to come. The church helped the family move out of the orchard and to the solid ground they desperately needed, and they continued to feed the family physically and spiritually.

One Sunday was all it took. One Sunday changed everything. The sister's life and the life of her family was never the same.

On the day I graduated from my doctoral program at West Virginia University and stood at the podium addressing the graduating class, I was reminded of this story, my own family history. In my address to the student body, I shared a quote from author and speaker Andy Andrews: "Don't squander your words or your thoughts. Consider even the simplest action you take, for your life and those lives you come in contact with matter beyond measure...and they matter forever."[2] I intentionally and specifically chose this quote from Andrews not just because I found it to be pithy or interesting, or a great moral proverb. His words did not describe something I knew just from a distance, but they described the impact others had on my family. My grandmother had to burn her baby doll for the family to stay warm.

There are many reasons why I believe that acts of caring carry greater impact than one may ever know. For one, acts of caring not only impact the person being cared for, but also impact the lives and trajectories of the generations that follow. I have never met anyone from that church who cared for my grandmother and her family, and at the same time their act of caring has profoundly impacted my life.

By the time I graduated from WVU, my grandmother had long been with Jesus, but I cannot help but think that even when my grandmother was living, she would not have imagined what would unfold in the years to come, that when she lived in that apple orchard and watched students walk by to the university, that one day her grandson would graduate from that same university and address the student body or even that several of her grandkids would also attend classes and look forward to their own bright futures.

The care that Jesus and the church family showed my family changed our history.

That's why we care for people. Even if we do not see the results or appreciation, caring demonstrates that each individual

belongs, matters, and is known. We care because caring restores dignity, helps someone
feel seen, impacts a person's trajectory, provides a self-inventory for the caregiver, and
ultimately caring changes us. Let's explore
each of these.

> The care that
> Jesus and the
> church family
> showed my
> family changed
> our history.

Caring Recognizes Dignity

Dignity is not a word I hear much about these days. On the contrary, I hear a lot about personal rights, personal perspective,
personal truth, and personal opinions. But dignity is about acknowledging the inherent value that is in each of us. Recognizing dignity is seeing and holding up the value of another simply
because they are human. Dignity is the impetus for caring.

My Christian faith influences my focus on dignity. I believe
that when Jesus died for humanity, He paid the same price for
each person. Every person has dignity because of the price paid
for them. They have value and worth because of the price paid.
Our worldviews may not agree here, and you are free to hold
your opinion, but I challenge you and raise you one homemade
apple pie with pecans and vanilla ice cream (now you know I'm
serious) to name another person who did more for human dignity than Jesus. Jesus changed society's perspective on the value
of women and children, the persecuted, those fallen from social
standing, those rejected by society, and those in need.

In the sight of God each person holds equal value. Regardless of what they own, what they do, who they know, and who
knows them. No matter their temptations, gifts, talents, physical abilities, or looks, everyone has significant and equal value
in God's eyes as they are created by Him in His image.

When someone cannot see their personal dignity because of their circumstances, our caring for them demonstrates that we see their God-given dignity. When we care for someone in their time of need, we show them their value. When I find myself walking through a difficult time, I often feel vulnerable, and in our day and age, society often takes advantage of the vulnerable. When we go countercultural and choose to care for the vulnerable, rather than take advantage, we help demonstrate and reinforce dignity rather than destroy it.

Caring Shows a Friend (or Anyone) They Are Valued

In our busy world, our friendships are often formed around and based on intersecting schedules. Where our lives and schedules intersect is where our relationships develop: people we work with, people we play sports with, people we attend church with, and people living in our community.

I am all for these relationships and believe they are natural, but what happens when our schedules no longer intersect due to life challenges? What happens when a person does not show up to work because she is sick? What happens to the guy on our softball team when he can no longer play because he needs to care for his sick parents? What happens when someone loses their job and stops coming to church as they wrestle with how God let that happen? What happens when your colleague is battling anxiety and depression during a pandemic and cannot get out of bed most mornings?

Often, we are so caught up in our own world that we move past another without noticing what has happened. But when we care for someone as they journey through life's challenges and let them know *more than once* that they are missed and that you care for them, they feel seen. It is hard for me to think of something that might heap hurt onto hurt more than when someone is in a challenging time and could use some help, but no one stops to offer it, leaving them to feel unseen, unknown, and unheard as if they and their life were not really that important after all. Most likely that's not true, but human logic is not always at its clearest in challenging times.

Men reading this, I have spent a significant part of the last 10 years working with our kind. I can see you squirming as your brain processes the words on these pages, thinking that this showing-that-you-care business is too touchy-feely. I submit that the reason for the discomfort is that for several generations, men have been out of touch with their emotions. We have emotions and feelings, but we do not know how to name them in a healthy way. We see emotions as unmanly. Men often seek reward and affirmation, but most men have not been rewarded, affirmed, or praised for feeling and acknowledging emotions. To the contrary. We are often criticized for showing emotions, so we work to repress them, put on a masculine front, and push on. But walking through a challenging time and feeling forgotten hurts, so men, let's demonstrate that we do care. Step up and find a way to communicate that you care, to show people in your life that they are seen, heard, and known in their challenging times.

Caring Impacts Trajectory

My nonscientific definition of trajectory is the direction an object moves due to the forces around it. Sometimes those forces are in our control; they are the result of decisions we make. At other times, someone or something else controls the force that impacts our trajectory.

I played baseball when I was young. As I grew up, I became progressively worse at the sport compared to my teammates and opponents, mostly because my vision steadily deteriorated. I simply could not see well. Eyeglasses would have been a big help, but I was too prideful to wear them. I was so resistant to the idea of wearing eyeglasses that I memorized the letters on the vision test at school by listening to everyone in front of me so that I could pass the test and not be required to get eyeglasses. But I could not memorize hitting or catching a baseball. I had to be able to measure the speed and trajectory of the ball in split seconds. The older I got, the poorer my vision got, and I just could not see the ball. It was hard to know where and when the little white ball coming my way at a high rate of speed was going to drop because I could not see it.

Just like I could not see the baseball's trajectory without glasses, there is no way for me to see my family's trajectory without the pastor and church family caring for my grandmother when she was a child in Morgantown, West Virginia. Without their caring force interacting with my grandmother and her family, does someone else come along and care at a later time? Are the children divided up and never see each other again? Are the children forced into less than desirable working conditions and taken advantage of? There are countless possibilities, and most outcomes probably would not include the stories of joy and grace that we now know. Each time I share the story of my family heritage and how the pastor and church cared for them, I am reminded of how those people who I never met were a caring force that impacted the trajectory of my life today.

> ∨
>
> **Acts of caring impact the lives and trajectories of the generations that follow.**

Caring for others is not a scientific or mathematic formula with inputs and outputs; we cannot calculate the trajectory of our caring force. Still, when we care for others, we *do* impact their trajectory physically, emotionally, and spiritually. Caring for someone can certainly impact their lives and the generations that follow.

Caring (or Not Caring) Requires a Self-Inventory

For the last couple years, on most mornings, I read Regi Campbell's devotional *Radical Wisdom*.[3] The other day it reminded me about self-inventories, a practice that I have found helpful. Regi includes the following questions in his self-inventories.

Have I become less kind and patient?

Nothing like starting off with an easy question, right? Am I noticing others and their challenging circumstances but not praying to see if God desires for me to act? Am I intentionally not listening to God and others because I do not want to know and feel responsible to care? Have I predetermined to not care because I made choices to fill my life up with so many other things that I don't have the time and space to care about anything else? Am I more concerned about being right than I am about the person who I am trying to convince that I am right? My answers to these questions give me insight into whether I am growing in my patience and kindness or becoming less patient and kind. My dad often says that it's never Christlike to be rude. Rudeness sums up a lack of patience and kindness. For sure there are days and hours that I am stressed, and my patience and kindness are not at their peak, but when I see a pattern of impatience and unkindness, I am far from who I desire to be.

Am I less forgiving?

Sometimes caring for others is not some grand act that takes time and money to accomplish. Forgiveness can be one of the greatest acts of caring that we can provide because true forgiveness cannot be bought with time or money. When I find myself falling into the fundamental attribution error of assigning motive, blaming, attacking someone else's character, and not forgiving them, I drift from care. I can quickly explain the reasons I deserve forgiveness and care, as well as how it was not my fault but rather the world's fault.

Caring for someone is swallowing the pain caused and forgiving them, rather than fighting to right the wrong. "Wisdom does not hurt the one who has hurt you. Wisdom breaks the pain cycle by being the hurt swallower.... Wisdom knows that the way for hurt to be healed is by absorption. Someone has to choose to swallow the pain rather than to pass it on."[4] When I swallow the injustice, I am caring and I am more forgiving.

Am I a good friend right now?

Another "ouch" question. Solomon, one of the wisest men who ever lived, wrote: "A friend loves at all times, and a brother is born for a time of adversity" (Proverbs 17:17 NIV). A friend loves at all times, even when it is not convenient. A friend is there when it is not fun, exciting, or personally beneficial. Am I being that type of friend? If I am being that type of friend, one who is there in times of good and plenty and times of bad and lack, on the mountaintop and in the valley, that is a sign that I am a good friend.

Am I present?

I add three words to the question: Am I present emotionally, spiritually, and physically? You have probably experienced being in a room or physically in someone's home but a long way away in your thoughts and emotions. Or you are right in front someone talking to them as they look past you, scoping out the room to see who else they really want to talk to. Or you are in a room with someone but are second fiddle to their phone.

This is the toughest question for me. In fact, the other three questions all hinge on this one. Being a true friend, being patient and kind, and being forgiving require my presence. Those who know me best would say that being truly present is probably one of the toughest things for me. When I conduct my self-inventory, I may fool myself on the first three questions, but I cannot fool myself or anyone else on this one.

Caring for others requires affirmative answers to each of these questions. I challenge everyone to ask themselves these questions or some form of them on a regular basis. If we truly desire to care for others, it is imperative to know how we are doing, and a quick self-inventory is a great place to start. Thanks, Regi!

Caring Changes Me/Us

The first time I really thought about and pondered this was as I sat at a table with people I had known for several years. We had been talking about life, family, faith, and work, and in the process of talking about some highs and lows, my friend made a statement I have thought about over and over: "I am glad you get to care for others because of the way it makes you feel."

At first, his statement offended me, and then I started to feel ashamed, that in some way his perception of me was that I only cared for others because it made me feel good. I bristled at the thought of this. Internally, I thought, "I don't care for others because of the way it makes me feel. I care for others because there is a need and I want to help care for them in their time of need." Yet, for some reason, I was not even satisfied with my own response. I felt like I was trying to convince myself, or some unseen jury, but was coming up short. Do I care for others because of the difference it makes in me?

My current conclusion is, yes, the changes that occur in me when I care for others are part of my motivation. They are not my only motivation, but they are definitely part of it.

When I was a kid, our family ventured to Virginia Beach most summers. My parents booked an oceanfront room so we could play at the beach from early morning to late in the afternoon. The only rule for the water was that my sisters and I needed to stay directly in front of the hotel. I loved to splash in the waves and body surf. I had watched the 1987 movie *North Shore* and dreamt of becoming the next great surfer. But as I played in the water and dreamt of being a surfer, I slowly and unconsciously drifted down the beach. The current pulled me a few feet every few minutes and before I knew it, I was 200 yards or so from where I needed to be. The waves pulled me without my realizing it until I looked up to find the hotel.

In the same way, I can go about my regular day and develop habits and routines that streamline my activities. In the process of those habits and routines, perhaps I convince myself that I am independent and quite capable of doing things on my own, drifting from the reality of how much I need God in my life. As I care for others, I realize how dependent I am on God for strength, discernment, and wisdom to keep from drifting, and that change in me is good.

As we care for others, we realize there are situations and challenges in life that we cannot handle on our own. We need God's help to navigate as we care for others. We need His help to find compassionate words to say and the actions that demonstrate that we truly care. I have found that when confronted with caring for others and the life challenges they face, even those who do not believe in God find a need for dependence on a higher power. Caring for others changes us as we recognize our dependence on a higher power.

Caring for others also changes me as I develop friendships and bonds that I would not have discovered any other way. Sometimes the relationships I build are with the person I am caring for, and other times it is with those I serve alongside (more the latter than the former). This is a real case of confirmation bias, but I see this all the time. Teams come to Africa to serve in a multiplicity of ways. People who do not know each other very well in their home country venture around the world to serve together and in the process make lifelong friends. It could be the travel, navigating a new culture, or simply the experience of being overseas, but I think it mostly comes from caring for others that forms the common bond and builds relationships.

As I traveled the rural areas of Madagascar, my initial goal was to care for the Malagasy people in areas with no access to healthcare. We traveled far and wide with planes, helicopters, hovercrafts, zebu carts, canoes, motorbikes, our own two feet, and the mobile clinic to accomplish our goal. In the process of caring for others, I built lifelong friendships, made memories, and captured good storytelling material. Caring for others changes us by giving us opportunities to build new relationships and strengthen existing ones.

Building relationships and recognizing our dependence on a higher power can be scary. No doubt about it, when we put ourselves out there, we risk hurt, humiliation, and disillusionment. To walk into these unsure situations takes courage, and caring for others gives us the opportunity to grow in courage. It is another way that caring for others changes us.

Finally, caring for others removes me from the center of my story. I find that I put myself at the center of every story, intentionally or not. My world becomes very small when it centers and rotates around me. By caring for others, I make conscious decisions to take the focus off myself, remove myself from the center, and focus on caring for someone else. The other person becomes the center of the story as I step aside. How refreshing it is when my small world expands and my perspective changes. Caring for others changes my self-centered heart.

DEVELOPING YOUR CARING LIFE

Perhaps my family's story and the generational impact of those who cared for them resonated with you. Most likely it resonated because you have a story of your own. The names and places in your story are different than mine, but someone impacted your life and your family.

With a desire to grow in a *caring life*, what role can you play in helping others see their God-given dignity? Are you willing to take the time to impact someone's trajectory? Are you courageous enough to see how caring for others will impact and change you? When it comes to life application, I have found one of the best places to start is self-examination. Following are some questions for you to consider, ponder over, and wrestle with:

Caring Recognizes Dignity

1. When did someone care for you in a way that helped you recognize the God-given dignity you hold?

2. What did they say or do that made you feel this way?

3. Have you cared for someone and recognized their value in God's eyes when they did not see it?

Caring Shows a Friend (or Anyone) They Are Valued

1. What are some reasons being seen is so valuable to the human condition?

2. Who has made you feel seen through their care?

3. Who can you care for that may feel forgotten or unseen in their time of need?

Caring Impacts Trajectory

1. What is your family's story when it comes to caring and trajectory?

2. Have you shared that story with others?

3. What are some reasons that you have or have not shared your family's story?

4. Who can you care for and help impact their trajectory?

Caring (or Not Caring) Requires a Self-Inventory

1. How does stress and living with little to no margin impact your patience and kindness?

2. What does "swallowing pain rather than passing it on" mean to you?

3. How can you be more present emotionally and spiritually?

Caring Changes Me/Us

1. How has caring for others changed you?

2. What are ways that caring for others takes the attention away from your world?

3. How do you feel about yourself when you care for others?

CHAPTER 2

The Art of Caring

I n the summer of 2004, I arrived in Ouagadougou (pronounced *waa-guh-doo-goo*), Burkina Faso, with my beautiful wife and 4-month-old daughter. Where in the world is Burkina Faso? I had no idea where it was until we were asked to live and serve there. I thought it was 100 percent in South America. No joke. Until a map of West Africa clearly identified its location. That was a humbling moment as I realized I had asked to move to a continent, but when offered a location on said continent, I had no idea it even existed. I learned many things in my West Virginia education, but evidently, African geography was not my strongest subject.

My family and I arrived in Burkina Faso after spending 10 months learning French in France. I have fond memories of France, but I am not a linguist by any stretch of the imagination. Trying to learn French was a challenging time for me and considerably more so when I realized, after six months of study, that the gender of words in French was not something I could fake my way through. Even if I had understood the importance of masculine and feminine words from the beginning and had the linguistic mechanics down, my West Virginia twang bleeds through. I never figured out if being told I spoke French better than a Spanish cow was an insult to the Spanish cow or an insult towards me. But I was young and excited to get on African soil and willing to do whatever it took, even if that meant making a fool of myself as I tried to speak French and was compared to a *vache espagnole*.

When we arrived in Burkina Faso, I thought communication would be my biggest challenge. Not even close. My biggest challenge came in the form of a tiny mosquito: *anopheles falciparum*. I learned mosquitoes might be small but when infected with malaria they pack a big punch. It became painfully obvious that I had good genetics in some areas, but malaria resistance was not one of them.

In our first days in Ouagadougou, the leaders of the church took me to the cemetery in town where 13 missionaries, of which seven are Americans, are buried. I am from Wiley Ford, West Virginia, and the son of a railroader, so direct communication is my comfort zone. But I was told that Burkinabe (those who call Burkina Faso their home) prefer indirect communication. That left me wondering what the message behind the trip to the cemetery was. Several thoughts ran through my mind for days after. Were they trying to say they had a burial plot there for me if I needed it; or they didn't know how long we'd make it and maybe I would be number eight for the Americans; or in retrospect, the most likely, I needed to respect those who went before me and paid the ultimate sacrifice and gave their lives.

In the days that followed that trip, my daughter Isabelle and my wife Heather both came down with malaria. We had done all we knew to do, but somehow all we did was not enough. Isabelle was diagnosed first. Heather and I were shocked and to be honest, downright scared. I was the last to test positive.

Heather and Isabelle made quicker recoveries, but I struggled over the next eight to 10 months and was actually diagnosed with malaria six times in that span. During that time, everything I wanted to do was greatly limited because I had very low energy and little to no stamina. When I did have energy, I spent much of my time being angry more than anything else. I was angry at the mosquitoes, the organization, leadership, and God. During those desert days, our organizational leader, Randy, was patient and kind with the frustrated and bull-headed young man from West Virginia. Because of my choice to hold onto anger directed at the organization, I resisted his genuine care for me and needed a voice from the outside.

I mentioned earlier that sometimes when we are looking for one thing or praying for a particular self-designed solution, God sends something else our way that fundamentally impacts our lives. My self-designed solution was leaning more and more towards a way out. Instead, God sent me someone to demonstrate the art of caring so that I could see leaving was not the solution. Staying and trusting God was. That person was Mark Lehmann.

I first met Mark through a God-designed encounter in Orlando, Florida. I didn't know him from Adam, but as Heather and I shared our burden and vision to serve specifically those with HIV/AIDS in Africa, the land of Heather's birth, the connection was undeniable. After that meeting in a hotel lobby, Mark invited us to live in Bowie, Maryland, for a year before we left for France. I was hesitant and had serious questions about this pastor I did not know who believed in us from the word "go." Sometimes when people believe in you more than you do yourself it can be unsettling—in a good way.

At the time, I had no idea how to categorize that meeting and tried to continue with life as usual, which meant going back to work at Lakeland Regional Medical Center. But that afternoon, the nurse supervisor came looking for me, saying there was a guy on the phone named Mark who wanted to talk to me.

Mark had tracked me down at the hospital. He called to touch base. He reiterated that he was serious about the offer. Having been around the church my whole life, I had a suspicion that he was looking for a janitor or something, but truly all he wanted to do was care for, invest in, and lock arms with us, which he and Cornerstone Church did during that one year before we headed to France (and have continued to do since).

Fast forward three years to Burkina Faso. In the middle of my desert moment both literally and figuratively, where self-doubt and God-doubt were palpable, Mark showed up. I had moved to Burkina Faso to care for those with HIV/AIDS but was in desperate need of someone who had a desire to care for me. Neither the malaria nor the heat nor the inconvenience deterred Mark. He had made his way across the ocean to sit, listen, encourage, and challenge me. In those days, Mark cared for Heather, Isabelle, and me, and ultimately demonstrated the art of caring that he has been gifted with and has developed.

From my nursing background, I was aware that nursing theorists, like Jean Watson,[5] often refer to nursing care as an art. Mark modeled that caring is not only an art form in nursing, but caring has much broader application. I was cared for during those days in the Sahel by someone who has truly been gifted with the art of caring and exercised that gift with excellence. He inspired me to do the same for others.

Caring as an Art Form

Some may be hesitant to call caring an art form. I understand. At times it is still a stretch for me. But before the idea is negated, at least consider it. My personal labeling of what is and is not art may be quite narrow and limiting. Frequently, when I think of the arts, I think of the paintings and sculptures in the Louvre or Musée D'Orsay, a masterful symphony performing at the Boston Philharmonic, an expertly executed play in a soccer match, or the tantalizing mountain ballad performed by John Denver entitled "Country Roads." (I might have lost you at "Country Roads." Do not hold it against me. #MountainMommaTakeMeHome)

Those with a similar view of art are in line with its common definition which refers to the various branches of imaginative activity like painting, sculpture, or dance that provide a visual expression of creativity. A more thorough definition includes the phrase "producing works to be appreciated primarily for their beauty or emotional power." I submit that anyone who has ever been on the receiving end of being truly cared for would find it hard to deny its beauty and emotional power.

∨

The quintessence of art is creating, and when caring is done well, it, too, is creative.

The quintessence of art is creating, and when caring is done well, it, too, is creative. I have never considered myself a creative person and have used that excuse in the past. I told myself that I am a logical thinker and work much better from a template rather than creating a template. For instance, I did great in math until I got to calculus.

Caring Takes Effort

In my senior year of high school, my friends Chris and Jason and I went to the local community college to take calculus. I remember my calculus professor describing the creativity needed to solve problems. Knowing formulas was only half the battle; knowing when and where to use them was the other. Calculus and I were never friends (maybe the first day of class, but it ended there). I could never get there creatively or mentally. After struggling with calculus, I thought I had proof that I was certifiably not creative.

For six years, I held on tightly to the idea that I had proof that I was not creative. Then one weekend I attended a conference that changed my perspective on my lack of creativity. I distinctly remember the room in Ocean City, Maryland, where Mark Batterson shared about being a pastor and writer, and about his passion for creative sermon preparation. I cannot remember what he said word for word, but he said something to the effect of: "Several of you in this room use the excuse that you are just not creative. But that is not the truth because we serve a creative God. It is only your excuse. Creativity takes work, time, and unbelievable effort. You may be using the excuse that you are not creative because you are not putting in the work that is necessary to be creative." He and Jesus spoke to me that day. My excuse for not being creative was more laziness than anything else.

I encourage anyone reading this who is like I was and has used the "I am not creative" line *and* used it as a reason to not step out and care for others to consider whether it is really the lack of creativity or the lack of will and work ethic to be creative in caring for others.

Caring Is Not Input-Output

Another reason I see caring as an art form is that caring is not an input-output relationship. I love input and output. I love science, math (well, not calculus), business; I am a numbers guy. But art forms are far from input-output. You could hand me the best paintbrush and paints and put me in a beautiful setting with the most expensive easel and canvas, and still my painting would not be much better than a kindergartener's. Painting by numbers is where my illustrious painting journey ended.

When I was six, my mom wanted me to play a musical instrument. She wanted me to have a talent I could use until I was old and grey. For several years I tried piano. The keyword is *tried.* In my first piano lesson, I was more interested in catching the guppies in the teacher's fish tank than learning to play "Yankee Doodle Dandy." After my first lesson, I was wet and although she was kind, I am certain my teacher was frustrated (though I did manage to land a few guppies and they survived the experience). I apologized at the next lesson, and I gave up on the guppies. I then tried and practiced piano for several years, but ladies and gentlemen, I have Vienna sausages for fingers. The piano was not my calling.

Some visions die hard, so in middle school I tried the trumpet. My parents bought the trumpet. I learned how to pucker my lips just right. Then I was told my lips were too big for the trumpet and I was better suited for the tuba. Finally, a few years later, everyone agreed maybe musical instruments were not my thing. The art of making music is not an input-output thing. If it was, I would be a pianist and a trumpeter.

Caring, like music, does not have an input-output correlation. If it did, it would be easier to master and results would be more certain. Caring takes more than inputs; it takes creativity as well as the ability and desire to listen, observe, and notice before responding. Maybe you have encountered someone trying to care for you, but they were really just going through the motions. Divorcing creativity from the art of caring produces hurt feelings and frustrations for both the person trying to care and the one requiring care.

Like other art forms, some individuals are simply gifted in caring for others. It comes easy for them. They are naturally inclined towards it. They can listen, see, and care for those around them. As for the rest of us, we can be jealous of them and their gifting and talent, or we can learn from them and the talent they have.

Caring Requires Action

And lastly, caring is an art form because caring requires action. The definition of art calls it activity. Creative thoughts are put into motion so they can be realized.

One of my college roommates was a music major. I remember walking into our room one day and saw him rapidly moving his fingers in the air. I asked him what he was doing. He said he was practicing the piano. Though my piano career was short-lived, I was pretty certain that playing the piano produced sound and that touching and feeling the keys was vitally important. But my creative roommate was convinced sound and piano keys were optional to the process; the motion and activity were enough.

Caring is an art because it requires action. Art is an activity (or activities) that produce something beautiful and emotionally moving. Our thoughts produce something as they are put in motion. I have been moved at times when somebody expresses the thought of caring for me, but I have been moved innumerable times when someone took their thoughts and put them into actions that produced something beautiful in my life.

When it comes to putting thoughts into action, I have more regrets than I can list here. I had opportunities to care and opportunities to put God's ideas into action, but I never progressed past the thought phase. I ran into barriers that I created or imagined, that I lazily gave into rather than fought through. We will look at some of these barriers in the next chapter.

So, are you almost convinced that caring is an art? Will you at least consider it? What Mark did in coming to Burkina Faso in my time of need was art. Hands down. Flying halfway around the world took putting thoughts into action. It was a visual expression of his caring for Heather, Isabelle, and me. It was a beautiful thing that still brings the emotion of gladness to the forefront and reminds me of the hurt, anger, and shame that I was deep into during those days. If not for Mark caring for me, it is hard to know exactly where I would be today. (I surely would not be authoring a book about caring.)

DEVELOPING YOUR CARING LIFE

Despite my best efforts and intentions, perhaps you are not convinced that caring is an art. All I can say is that I tried. Agreeing with me on this is not the biggest point. The key in this chapter is to recognize that caring is something that we can grow and develop in. Following are questions that can help you process how you view caring and whether you view it as an art:

Caring as an Art Form

1. Do you consider yourself artistic?

2. If you do consider yourself artistic, how can you apply these creative principles in how you care for others?

3. If you do not consider yourself artistic, how can you grow in your creativity so that you can apply it to caring?

Caring Takes Effort

1. Do you consider caring for others work? Does this change who you are caring for and when?

2. How can you create, conserve, or guard energy so that you can use it to care for others?

3. What are some ways you can resist the drift towards not putting in any creative effort in your care for others?

Caring Is Not Input-Output

1. Have you cared for someone but did not see the results you thought you would see? What did you learn from this experience?

2. How can you grow in your understanding and application that each of us is responsible for our inputs but cannot be responsible for the outputs?

3. Are you willing to care for others if you are not guaranteed the outputs or results you desire to see?

Caring Requires Action

1. Have you ever had an opportunity to care for someone but did not put your thoughts into action? How did it make you feel? Did you regret it?

2. What are some steps you can take to move your caring thoughts to caring actions?

3. Who have you observed that puts thoughts into action that you can learn from?

CHAPTER 3

Barriers to Care

After living in Burkina Faso and surviving the mosquitoes and malaria, my family and I moved to Madagascar. Living and working in Madagascar provided fewer opportunities for malaria and plenty of opportunities for adventure, but anyone who knows me knows that I am not the most adventurous guy. I prefer controlled environments over the unknown. The "let's see what happens" type of situations are not for me. (Thus, the reason I drifted away from the emergency room and the psychiatric care unit towards dermatology.) But living in Madagascar would require adventure as I knew God called me to care for the medical needs of those who lived in remote areas of the island. So, adventure it was as we traveled the big Red Island.

When we first arrived in Madagascar, I was looking for things to do. I am not good at sitting still *and* it is usually not good for anyone around me when I am sitting still. Enter adventure number one. A group of guys with more experience living and serving on the island invited me to join them, and I was to provide medical care in the villages we visited. We were traveling to the west coast to an area that was not (and still is not) well controlled by the government. Which means whoever has the biggest or the most guns is in control.

This was my first of many trips to an area where I now have many great stories and memories. On this trip, we traveled by helicopter as the location was not accessible by road. The first thing I thought as I looked at the landscape was, "I'm not in Wiley Ford, West Virginia, anymore." The villages where we worked were on one side of a large, knee-deep river.

Once the helicopter set down and the engines were off, the local Malagasy cordially greeted us. They welcomed us to set up our camp near their village so we were protected from the raiding bandits that plagued that side of the river. (Somehow, I missed the "raiding bandits" part of the invitation when I was asked to come and provide medical care to those living in these villages.) The guys I was with, however, did not miss a beat. I followed their lead.

It was *hot* in the village, and the sound of beating drums could be heard in the distance. It was a time of celebration as a local chief's first son had been born that day. Those in the village danced around in happiness. The guys in the group decided to join the festivities and removed their shoes and stripped off their clothes. They put on a cloth that covered their mid-section, dressed like the villagers, and began to celebrate. I just kept asking myself, "What have I gotten into?" It felt like I was in the Christian version (if there could be one) of the TV reality show *Naked and Afraid*. I did not strip down or remove my shoes, so this was more like *Almost Naked and Somewhat Afraid*. Fresh off my experiences with malaria, I knew one way to prevent mosquito bites was to stay covered.

We then proceeded to set up camp. I was a Royal Ranger[6] growing up, but my camping skills were rusty, to say the least.

I had bought a new tent for this special occasion so I could look the part, and I decided to set it up under a giant mango tree thinking it would provide cover and shade. Unfortunately, what I did not know was that the flying foxes (think big bats) loved to return to the tree each night to eat the green mangoes. And mangoes they ate and ate. It was a mango buffet for all the flying foxes in the tree. Throughout the night, I heard them crunching on the mangoes and dropping the seed which frequently hit my tent with a thud. From the resulting poop fest that painted my brand-new tent, I deduced mangoes eaten in high quantities are hard on the digestive tract of flying foxes.

In addition to flying foxes' love for mango trees, I did not realize my tent was not truly waterproof. We had amazing downpours in the evenings. The rain came and came, and if my tent had not been staked in the ground, it and I might have floated away. There was easily two inches of water in my tent on two nights of the trip. (The rain did clean the flying fox poop off the tent; that's a positive.)

But the best part was not the flying foxes and mangoes or the not-so-waterproof tent. One night the bandits paid a visit to our camp, carrying their guns and making their threats. They were known for stealing cattle, burning villages, and killing anyone who tried to prevent them from doing what they came to do. Seeing a bunch of foreign men in the middle of nowhere, I guess they thought we were an easier target than most.

I had not encountered bandits like these before. They seemed nicer than the typical bandits. They gave fair warning of what they planned to do and via a local translator proceeded to tell us exactly what they wanted from us. We could either hand it over or they would come back and steal it. They were polite bandits. My Malagasy was limited at the time, but I could hear the interpreter translating between the bandits and our team leader. The bandits made their threats and postured for the things they wanted. Their guns and machetes were enough to convince me.

Our team leader was braver than I, and I quickly learned he was an excellent bluffer. As the bandits made their threats, he told them about all the weapons hidden in our tents. Weapons? I had zero weapons and knew the others did not have any, other than a few Leatherman tools. The team leader shared we were there to serve the communities with medical care and the good news of Jesus, and we would not be threatened by them and their guns. If they really wanted a fight, we would defend ourselves to live another day.

Wait a minute. I was there to care for the local villagers, not fight bandits with my nonexistent weapons that even if they did exist, I would have no clue how to use them. Thankfully, the bandits were convinced that this group of half-naked guys were not the fight they were looking for that night and left us alone.

Most of our opportunities to care for someone are not filled with near as much excitement or adventure as flying foxes, downpours of rain, or polite bandits. But there still are common barriers to truly caring for those we know or those we hear about who are in need of care.

Being Inattentive

The first barrier that hinders us from caring for others is inattentiveness. Simply stated, we find what *we* are looking for and see what *we* are focused on. Life challenges are rarely ever scheduled or planned, and most of us move at such a fast pace that we blow by people because we get so focused on our schedule rather than on people.

Those who work in the caring profession can attest to this. They are specialists at paying attention, and even the specialists have to concentrate on noticing. Nurses, doctors, pastors, counselors, and coaches could share story after story of people who have been hurt by others' inattentiveness.

Think about the last difficult time you faced or maybe one you are currently facing. Most likely it was unexpected, not planned, and you were forced to pay attention, slow down, or at least change speed and focus. Due to the pace and lack of space in our lives, our attentiveness is rarely ready for the unexpected. We move at hectic speeds and more and more our lives are built around the convenient and fast. Do not get me wrong. I am all for conveniences, and honestly, I drift towards choosing them. But caring for people rarely ever happens to be the most convenient choice.

Conveniences are possible, in part, due to advances in technology, which are happening at a lightning pace. John Maxwell wrote that fast has never been faster and that the future will never be slower because the digital world will not accept anything but faster and better.[7] He further noted that one effect of this faster digital age is that the future is shorter and closer than it ever has been.

The idea of the future being closer propels us into a furious pace of life. With faster lives built with little to no margin, we have little space to care for others. Meaning when someone is sick, a friend is facing trouble in their marriage or at work, an employee who you serve cannot keep pace because they have a sick loved one, or a neighbor is struggling to find a job, we have pretty much pre-determined that we will not have time in our schedules to stop and care for them. I do not think it's because we do not care. It's just that we have chosen convenience. We have chosen inattentiveness. We do not have the time to stop and listen, let alone, stop long enough to listen *and* care.

How do we battle the inattentiveness fueled by the speed of life, which then hinders us from caring? How can we battle and overcome it? Author Adam McHugh provides some great first steps. His book *The Listening Life* really hit home for me. Those who desire to grow in their attentiveness, listening is a great place to start. In the book, McHugh challenges his readers to listen as Jesus did. Maybe you are not a Jesus follower, but I believe we can all learn from the way Jesus listened.

Before we jump into three things McHugh says we can do in our listening, I want to stress the power and the importance of listening in caring. It is nearly impossible to care for someone without first listening to them, observing the situation, or hearing their hearts. I am guilty of having skipped this vital step. Rather than listening, I just give a solution to what I think someone's challenge is. I learned early on to never do this in a professional setting. For instance, if someone comes into the dermatology office, I never say, "I see you are here for your acne" or "I see you are here because your nose is all swollen from your rosacea." *Big mistake.* Oftentimes, what seems to me the obvious reason someone has come in is *not* the reason they came in to see me. *Or* they have come using one reason to see if they can trust me before sharing the real reason. So, my two questions always are: What has brought you in today? How can I help care for you?

The first of three things we can do to beat back inattentiveness is *listen first*. McHugh shares that Jesus demonstrated true listening as a profound act of hospitality. He demonstrated the power of presence. Jesus wanted to be close so He could listen. Jesus gave His full attention to people. He did not interrupt what they were saying, and He never listened with one ear. When the woman was healed by touching His garment, He was not content to let it go. He wanted to meet the woman—not so He could take the glory, but so she could feel known. He desired to listen to her so she could feel known, valued, and cared for. Jesus listened with His whole self. Jesus was fully present.

Are we fully present when we are listening? For example, I find it distracting when I am listening or being listened to and the other person glances at their phone. It breaks the power of presence as the outward action shows a glimpse of the inward distraction.

Secondly, McHugh shares that Jesus *listened widely*. Perhaps the most interesting thing is not *how* Jesus listened but *who* He listened to. I admit that due to my inattentiveness if I fail to listen to those close to me, I most likely am not listening to anyone at all. Jesus had a habit of listening to people others ignored: the poor, the sick, the foreigners, the sinners, even His enemies. Imagine in today's culture if we truly listened to those who do not see the world the way we do.

McHugh writes that many religious people of the day were so occupied with being the voice of God, they were unable to hear those who *seemed* far away from them. It is interesting that Jesus did not often listen to those who thought they had a *right* to be heard but dropped everything to listen to children who came with no pretense or conception that they were important enough to be heard. I pray that we are like Jesus, learning to listen to those who do not look, think, or act as we do. Are we willing to battle inattentiveness by listening widely?

Finally, McHugh pointed out that Jesus *listened deeply*. Jesus could hear what was unsaid. He paid attention to body language and gestures. He could read people's faces. When we read the

Bible, we see that Jesus at times responded to a question with a question and used questions to dig deeper. McHugh shares that when Jesus interacted with the teachers of the law and their question about how to inherit eternal life, Jesus responded with a question that allowed Him to see deeper and see what was truly going on in the teachers' hearts.[8]

My struggle: I am very quick to search for an answer to someone's question. That is what I have been rewarded for most of my life: not for asking good questions and listening, but for giving the right answers. As leadership expert Steve Cuss has helped me understand, I feel the anxiety build inside me until I can come up with an answer to someone's question. Jesus was not always quick to respond to a question with an answer. Instead, by listening, Jesus revealed underlying needs. He was rarely (maybe never?) interested in surface or superficial conversations. By listening deeply, He demonstrated a true heart of caring.

Feeling Incompetent

Our lack of attentiveness has led to a lack of experience in caring for others. We have fallen out of practice when it comes to truly caring for anyone other than ourselves. The more I do something, the more my confidence builds. For instance, I cannot tell you how many times I have learned to read an EKG (electrocardiogram). Countless times. The problem lies in that I care for people facing skin challenges, not heart challenges. If you need an EKG read, I am not your guy. Rash, yes. Heart problem, no.

If we do not exercise our care muscles, they atrophy. Maybe the reason we feel incompetent in caring is that we want the "professionals" or the government or the church to care for our friends, neighbors, employees, or colleagues. But this is not a them-or-me option; it's both/and. With evaluative experience comes further competence and growth as we grow our care muscles.

You might not believe that caring for others is your thing. You might believe that you are not gifted to care for others. Maybe you are not gifted in the art of caring, but you do not get a free pass to not care or to just care in "thoughts and prayers" and heart emojis.

Brett Johnson's work and book on Convergence and the importance of understanding our natural talents, acquired abilities, and our spiritual giftings speaks to all of us. Natural talents, he says, are things you are born with, something that was recognized in you from the time you were little. I loved playing basketball and it came naturally to me. Singing, not so much. I always wanted to be a singer (and maybe I could have been), but I did not have the natural talent or ability to hear if I was singing on-key or off-key. Each person has natural talents, but maybe caring does not come naturally to you. I do understand this.

> **If we do not exercise our care muscles, they atrophy.**

But just like some are naturally talented in athletics or music or any other number of things, some people are just naturally talented at caring for others. Listening, observing, and responding come naturally to them. These people have the keen ability to see through and read between the lines of questions people are asking or areas in which they are struggling. They can see beyond the presented front and see the true challenge a person is facing.

There are a unique few that care deeply for others and at times cannot grasp why others do not care the way they do. But there are way too many people in need of care for those unique few to care for on their own. This is where those who do not have the natural talent of caring come in. According to Johnson, our acquired abilities are those skills we have grown in through training or studying. Those not born with the natural talent of caring for others can learn to care for others through mentorship, growth, practice, and study. That might be one of the reasons you are reading this book: You desire to grow in your ability to care for others. I think the majority of us fall into this category.

Christians also believe that when each person surrenders their heart to Jesus, they receive unique spiritual giftings—giftings specifically chosen by God for them. I know people who when they gave their heart to Jesus became some of the most sensitive and caring people one could ever meet. Maybe this is you, and you have been gifted later in life with a spiritual gifting of caring for others.

Whether you have a natural talent for caring, or you need to learn how to care for others, or God has gifted you later in life, you have no excuse to say you cannot care for others. The challenge for some of you will be to find someone who knows or is learning how to care for others. Find them, take them out for breakfast, and ask a lot of questions. It will be the best money you have spent in a while.

Feeling Overwhelmed

Caring for others might be easier if our lives were perfect, if we had no challenges, hurts, concerns, or limps of our own. But each of us has our own personal struggles that we carry into our present situations.

I can be overrun at times with all that is happening in my life and family which makes the thought of caring for someone else discouraging from the get-go. I have used all my fuel and I am running on fumes just to get through my day. On top of my own personal challenges is the constant barrage of news and social media of mostly uninspiring, deflating content. Combine these two and I am just overwhelmed. I am definitely not arguing that the feeling of being overwhelmed is not real or a figment of the imagination or made up. I am not negating it or trying to prove that it does not exist. Because I am with you. It does exist. And living in this paralysis of being overwhelmed adds more pain and hurt to the world.

How do we combat the feelings of being overwhelmed? Exiting our family, work, neighborhood, church, or community is not really a viable option, nor a healthy one I might add. If these environments are toxic or abusive, that is another thing entirely, but a majority of them are not. If they are not toxic or abusive, exiting them is not really an option. So, what can we do? We can control the external content that we allow into our minds and hearts. The things we choose to dwell on are in our control. This is not a new concept or revolutionary idea, but some of the best ideas are not new and revolutionary. Since we were small, we were told, "Be careful little eyes what you see. Be careful little ears what you hear." We seem to forget this message the older we get, deciding it does not apply after we reach a certain age.

Some of my personal practices may help you here. My "firsts" are important. I am a morning person, so how I begin my day has a dramatic effect and impact on the rest of my day. I strive to only listen to and read certain content before 8 a.m. I first want music, devotions, and communication that will fill me up for the day. That means no social media until after my devotions and well after 8 a.m. No sports podcasts until after I have listened to my Spotify playlist or inspiring message. This might sound a little legalistic to you. It is not legalistic for me. It is the way I have found to increase my ability to truly care for others. These are the proven practices and choices that I make to give me the bandwidth to care for others.

Beyond the morning, I became vigilant about what I allow my eyes to see and ears to hear through the media. This is easier said than done. I am not suggesting you block out the world, but I also know that many people have enough physical hurt and wounds around them that cutting back media time would be of great value. I have enough drama and stories in my own small world that I cannot continually and habitually take in endless amounts of the same from others around the world.

I challenge you to start measuring how you feel before and after you check out your favorite media outlet. Keep a running list on your phone or go old school and use a pen and paper. Before you take in media, take an inventory of how you feel. Start by writing down the primary emotions you are feeling (glad, hurt, sad, fear, shame, guilt, and lonely). When you finish taking in the content, return and write down what you feel. Want to get serious about it? Ask a family member or trusted someone to share what they see in you before and after. I have a few people in my life that I can tell when they have been looking at a screen too long. Their voice, face, and actions reflect it. You will be surprised about how social media in general impacts your emotions. Being vigilant with our intake will dramatically affect our overwhelmedness.

Doing for One

Another idea, popularized by author and pastor Andy Stanley, is to do for one what you wish you could do for everyone. The idea being that if we try to care for everyone, we will be overwhelmed, so rather than being overwhelmed and doing nothing, we can each invest time, energy, and money in caring for one person/one family. We can listen widely and deeply and be present in one situation a lot easier than we can in 10 different ones.

My challenge in doing for one what I wish I could do for everyone is how to select the one person to care for. Maybe it seems easy to just pick a person, but I am not a random type of person and God doesn't rely on luck. I believe in God moments and desire to walk in His guidance, so how do I separate my emotional reactions from the faith-filled responses? Faced with this challenge, I looked for a decision-making model that could help me process how to pick the one and not give into decision fatigue that would result in me not caring for anyone. Author, podcaster, and leadership expert Stephen Blandino is a friend, and he has a decision-making model that has helped me tremendously.

Do for one what you wish you could do for everyone.

God: *Provides Holy Spirit wisdom*

1. Have I prayed: "God, You see what is in front of me. Please give me the wisdom and knowledge that I need and the courage to pursue it if it is Your will"?

2. Have I invited God into the process of deciding to care?

Without God, my decision to care will lack supernatural influence.

DNA: *Provides consistency*

1. Does this situation align with my DNA?

2. Will this pull me in a direction that is contrary to who I am?

3. Does the need for care correspond to my gifting and talents?

Without DNA, my decision will lack consistency.

Research: *Provides depth*

1. Have I done my homework on this situation?

2. Have I asked questions and sought to understand what is happening and how I can care?

3. Have I investigated my heart to see if my motives are pure?

Without research, my decision to care may be an emotional one that I do not understand.

Advice: *Provides perspective*

1. Have I asked those wiser than me what they see and think?

2. Have I sought to learn from others before jumping in?

3. Am I open to learning from others?

Without seeking advice, my decision might be made without knowing my blind spots.

Past experience: *Provides maturity*

1. What have I personally learned in the past that will help me care today?

2. What has worked and what has not worked as I have cared for others?

3. What have I learned from others' experiences in caring that will help me today?

Without considering past experience, mine and others, my decision to care can lack maturity.

Influencers: *Provides buy-in*

1. Are those closest to me supportive of me caring?

2. Who will be most affected by my decision to care in this situation? What are their thoughts?

3. How will those closest to me be impacted by me caring for someone else?

Without influencers, my decision to care may sideline those closest to me.

Intuition: *Provides peace*

1. What is my gut telling me?

2. Am I listening to the nudges of the Holy Spirit?

Without intuition, I will not be at peace with my decision to care.

Timing: *Provides impact*

1. Is the timing right for the person I want to care for?

2. Is the timing right for me?

3. Is the timing right for my family?

4. Do I have the time to truly care, or will caring be out of duty?

Without timing, my care may not be meeting the need at the right moment for those involved.

I have found that running through these eight steps helps provide wisdom on deciding who the one is rather than walking into a situation with great intentions but with eyes wide shut.

Experiencing Hurt

When I was a kid, I was not always the most obedient. Some lessons I had to learn the hard way to know that I did not want to repeat them. One such lesson happened in the fifth grade. My friends and I liked to play cops and robbers on our bikes.

To be a good cop or a great robber, you needed the element of surprise on your side. I often hid in my neighbor's driveway because it provided the perfect amount of surprise when I came zooming out of the driveway. The only issue was that I could not see oncoming traffic until I reached a point of no return—the location that made it such a great point of attack also made it very dangerous. If a car was at a close distance, I was clearly in a bad spot. I would have to put the bike down and slide or, well, there were not really any other options.

My parents warned me many times about this, but I thought my reflexes and speed could get me out of a tight jam. (I'm sure you see where this going.) One day I came out of the driveway and found myself face to face with an oncoming car. I put the bike down and slid, but it was too late. The driver had no chance. The car's front tires ran over my legs and midsection and then spun me around. All I could think was, I am dead. Not from the car. My parents were going to kill me. I jumped up and ran looking for my dad to explain what had happened and to promise that, if he did not kill me, I would never do it again.

He did not kill me. In fact, he didn't even say, "I told you so." There was no need for that. The message was loud and clear. I never came out of that driveway again because of the pain I experienced on that day. Mentally, emotionally, and physically. I had dreams and nightmares about it. I realized how bad it really could have been. I did not like the pain and did not like the fear that it provoked, so I avoided it from that point on.

Unfortunately, many of us have been hurt, sometimes deeply, when we have attempted to care for someone else. If you have ever decided to care for someone, there is a high probability you were hurt in the process. Oftentimes, the hurt inflicted is not intentional, and I truly believe the majority of people are not nefarious. But I am sure you have heard it said that hurting people hurt people, and the hurt they feel is not just transferred to you or those around you but is often amplified and magnified. This transference of pain to the one who is trying to care is discouraging, frustrating, and deeply hurtful.

We associate caring with the pain we received from doing it. Just like me and the bike-driveway experience—I avoided the bike in that driveway because of the pain it caused. One way to avoid the pain is to not risk caring again. We build walls around our hearts, and to be overcautious, we add a moat in case there are any good climbers. We want to avoid the pain at all costs.

I wish there was an easy answer or a pithy solution, but I have not found one yet. When we decide to care for others, it comes with the knowledge that we just might, and probably will, get hurt in the process. That is why I think this is one of the biggest barriers to care. Because unless one is a masochist, one does not intentionally inflict pain on oneself.

Measuring Results

I have been in school more years of my life than not. I like the formal process of learning and the sense of measured achievement. I am not sure which one I prefer more or if I can even separate them.

For a long time, I felt a certain level of shame about my desire to achieve and see growth, but I have come to accept that in certain areas achievement is just part of who I am. I like to see results, and most of the time, I like to see results quickly. That is one reason I love to mow grass and wash dirty dishes because in both cases, I see the results of my time and effort quickly.

Yet, the "quick" part is a continual stumbling block for me in caring for others. Seeing the needs and challenges around me can provoke a sense of anxiety in me, and when I am anxious, I get impatient. I want to engage in something; I want to work, serve, and see the impact that can be made by caring. But my *caring life* is not an area that I commonly see quick results. I have struggled with that, with wanting to see results and improvement.

One of the best examples of this played out in Madagascar as I cared for my kids' physical needs. The medical care on our side of town was not the best, but it was vitally important that parents with sick kids had confidence in the person caring for their children, and so I was honored to provide a good bit of physical care for the kids in our expat community. In that scenario, I could remain objective and patient, trusting in prayer and our bodies' design to heal.

But when it came to my own kids, I was the physical, at-home caregiver as well, and my patience was dismal. Caring for someone else's child and sending them home to see them back in a few days was one thing, but when it was my child coughing, sick, and feverish, and I was seeing them hour by hour and minute by minute. I needed to see results. (This is one reason my kids received way too many medications growing up. Sorry, Isabelle and Josiah.)

Recall the story about my family. The pastor and those in the church witnessed some of the change, but they were not alive to see the generational impact they made. I am glad they did not give in to the desire to see immediate results. They pushed through this barrier to caring, and I pray I continue to push through it, too.

How can we overcome this desire to see quick results when we care for others? I started asking myself two questions. The first is: Am I willing to care for others even if I never see an impact from caring? The second is: What is my motive for caring for others? Throughout my life and in different seasons, my answers to these two questions have ranged broadly. But as I grow in maturity, I am more convinced that I am willing to care and leave the results to someone else. Do you let the need to see quick results hinder you from caring for others?

Encountering Complexity

Caring for other people can be quite complex. At times, caring for others can feel like solving a Rubik's Cube, in which turning one direction affects another direction and so on. There is little doubt that when we care for others we battle competing values, competing demands for our time and attention, and the reality that we can never make everyone happy all the time. Making everyone happy all the time is an impossibility. I have tried and it has surely not worked for me.

Is the complexity of caring a problem to be solved or a fact to be coped with? A former Israeli prime minister and president, Shimon Peres said, "If a problem has no solution, it may not be a problem, but a fact—not to be solved, but to be coped with over time." When it comes to caring and complexity, I have determined that caring in our day will only become more complex, and I desire to muster the courage to enter the complicated and complex situations that God leads me into, rather than run from them. I do not want complexity to create a fear in me that leads me to choose not to care. Anyone can do easy, but who will take on the complex?

Each of us will make a decision when it comes to caring and the barriers that stand in the way. My prayer is that each of us will grow in our tenacity and perseverance and not give into inattentiveness, past hurtful experiences, feeling incompetent or overwhelmed, or complexity.

DEVELOPING YOUR CARING LIFE

Our world is filled with reasons not to care. In this chapter I discussed a few with which I frequently struggle. If we do not reflect on the barriers that commonly hinder us from caring, then it is likely we will be a victim of them in the future. Following are questions that can help you explore the barriers of care that we run up against:

Being Inattentive

1. What are distractions in your life that prevent you from being attentive to others and not caring for them?

2. Would those closest to you call you a listener that listens widely, deeply, and intentionally so that you can better care for them?

3. How can you grow in your listening skills? What plan can you have to focus on those in front of you rather than those who are not present?

Feeling Incompetent

1. What are your natural talents?

2. What are your acquired abilities?

3. What are your spiritual giftings?

4. How can you use all three of these to care for others?

Feeling Overwhelmed

1. What are things in your life that add to you feeling overwhelmed? How does the overwhelming make you feel?

2. What is your morning routine? Does it increase or decrease the overwhelming?

3. How has being overwhelmed impacted how you care for others? Is there anything you can adapt or change?

Doing for One

1. In the past, how have you chosen who to care for? How has it worked out?

2. Is there a way you could use Stephen Blandino's model to help choose the "one"?

3. What is one step in the decision model that you might struggle with? How can you overcome this challenge and not give into inaction?

Experiencing Hurt

1. Have you been hurt when someone did not respond to your care as you thought they would?

2. Does such past pain make you less interested in caring for others?

3. How can you learn from the past hurt, but not let it prevent you from caring for others?

Measuring Results

1. Do you attempt to measure results when you care for others?

2. What are some reasons that measuring results has become so important?

3. Are you willing to care for others even if you never see the impact of your actions?

Encountering Complexity

1. Have you experienced the complexity that comes from caring for others?

2. How does complexity impact your desire to care for others?

3. Do you believe that complexity is something you can overcome so that you can care for others?

CHAPTER 4

A Caring Life and Self-Awareness

Arriving in Madagascar, I had certain ideas on how the rural clinics I would serve in would function. I had mental images of what they looked like. I pictured myself and someone else sitting in the back of the mobile clinic caring for those who were not well. I fully expected obstacles and challenges, but the obstacles and challenges I faced were nowhere close to what I imagined. Most of my mental images and ideas never came to fruition because they were based on ideas and images that lacked the context of the reality of life in rural Madagascar.

On a trip to a new part of the island, one I had not visited before, many of my ideas that had not yet faded quickly dissipated. After a long journey, we arrived in the village late in the day and spent the evening getting to know the villagers. We spent time with the village leader asking for permission to care for those in the area. The villagers were very kind and hospitable to us and went out of their way to make us as comfortable as possible.

We had brought tents to stay outside under the stars, but the village leader did not like that idea. He preferred that we stay in a 15-foot by 10-foot mud-walled building in the center of the village. He had two reasons for choosing this place: The first was the low metal roof to protect us from the rain so we wouldn't get wet, and the second was that it served as a barrier and shield from the local sorcerer that roamed the countryside.

The village leader told us that the sorcerers in this area of Madagascar were commonly women, highlighting that they were naked and covered in pig grease so they could not be caught or captured. The sorcerers came out at night to put curses on people by rubbing their pig-greased bodies up against them. He explained that our tents did not provide much of a barrier, but the mud-brick walls worked just fine. While I had never heard of such a thing and was not afraid of the sorcerer, the idea of a naked pig-greased lady rubbing against me in the middle of the night did not sound appealing. We kindly accepted his offer to stay in the building.

One nice thing about the rural areas, there is commonly no electricity. When the sun goes down, it is dark. I mean dark. We were exhausted from the day's journey and decided to go to bed early. There was a problem though: The rats living in our building were just waking up. One pastor on the trip had brought his guitar and propped it up against the wall near me. That night I experienced rats playing the guitar for the first time ever. I am accustomed to the sound of rats running on the roof and walls, and as long as they do not touch me, I'm good. That night, the rats used the guitar as a bridge to go up and down the wall, and every time they ran over the strings of the guitar, it sounded like someone badly strumming it. It woke me up many, many times throughout the night.

After the rats serenaded us for much of the night, we woke up to a line of sick people outside the building—and there were a lot of people who wanted to be seen. We quickly ate breakfast and started to see those waiting in line.

My training in caring for people and diagnosing their health challenges revolves around asking a series of questions commonly referred to as OLD CART. OLD CART is a mnemonic that stands for: onset, location, duration, characteristics, aggravating factors, relieving factors, treatments. It gives a clear path to follow when asking questions to figure out what is going on with someone. The next time you are at the nurse practitioner's office listen to see if they use it, too.

I started asking questions about the onset of symptoms and noticed that after four or five questions, the person put their head down and began to shake it back and forth. It happened with the first five or six people we cared for, so I finally asked the Malagasy doctor, Fils, who I was serving with, what the problem was. He shared that the villagers were discouraged and thought I did not know what I was doing because I had to ask so many questions to figure out what was causing their problem. They told him the local witch doctor only needed to ask three questions to figure out their illness, but the "doctor vahaza" had to ask so many questions because he did not know what he was doing.

I was somewhat disappointed and shared with him the reason why I was asking so many questions, that there was no way I could figure out what was causing their problem by asking three questions. I was starting broad and narrowing in on how I could care for them. Fils understood completely and tried to share this with those we were caring for. But they were not convinced and told Fils he was trying to cover up for the new doctor who had good-tasting medicine but who did not know what he was doing.

Caring and Self-Awareness

This chapter looks at a *caring life* and self-awareness through the lens of the Enneagram. For those not familiar, the Enneagram uses a questionnaire to help you grow in self-understanding. No questionnaire can tell you who you are completely, but the Enneagram can give insight into some of your tendencies. The different types in the Enneagram system correspond with the numbers 1 to 9. Perhaps you have heard people say, "I am an 8" or "that's a typical 2 for you."

There are numerous types of questionnaires, long and short, free and paid, valid and invalid. Free ones commonly share the 1 to 9 number at the end of the questionnaire so the person can research the tendencies associated with that type. Paid versions will give a number and a tool to better understand that type, and frequently share growth areas without the additional research required by the free versions. A valuable part of the paid versions is they provide information on how to interact in a healthy way with other Enneagram types and share how different types interpret each other.

For those who do not yet know their Enneagram type, most questionnaires you choose will at least provide the number and description that corresponds with your type, and this number will give you some insight into your tendencies and how you respond and react to those around you. If you go deeper into the Enneagram, the numbers are divided into the triads—gut, heart, and head—and these triads help demonstrate relationships and commonalities among the different types.

Full disclosure: I have my doctorate in nursing, which has its ethos in caring, and a master's in business administration, but I do not have a degree in psychiatry, psychology, counseling, or mental health. Although I have used and studied the Enneagram for the last five years, I am not an expert on the psychology or brain science behind it, but I do have practical experience in using it with teams as we strive to better care for each other. I have found it very valuable in helping myself and

> The Enneagram can be valuable tool to help you and I care for others.

others understand how various types impact the care we give and receive from each other. Most of what I have learned is from Ian Cron and Chuck DeGroat and I credit them both with much of my understanding of the different types. That said, I am writing from everyday relational experience and not as an authority on all things Enneagram and the psychology behind it.

Application

Before we look at the Enneagram numbers applied to a *caring life*, here is the application to my story from the bush of Madagascar. The villagers believed the witch doctor needed three questions to figure something out while I needed a plethora of questions to figure out the same thing. A questionnaire like the Enneagram is a valuable tool, but I find it descriptive rather than prescriptive. We may get a good idea about someone through a questionnaire, long or short, but to truly know someone takes more than looking at a number and drawing a conclusion from it. Perhaps you disagree and I respect that.

I have found that some people love the Enneagram and identify with their Enneagram number. They use this tool for healthier relationships. But like many things that one group loves, there are others who want nothing to do with the Enneagram and bristle at the idea that a number or word can be used to sum up their uniqueness. Some struggle with its history. I am somewhere in the middle; I believe it is one tool among several that we can use to understand ourselves and others better so we can effectively care. This particular tool helps me see tendencies in myself and others so I can care in a way that someone will feel cared for, and it helps me set my expectations on how they might receive and respond to my care. I am not someone who shares my Enneagram number and then proceeds to tell others they will have to accept it and deal with who I am. Our Enneagram number is not a weapon to be used against others; rather, it is something that helps us grow towards health and wholeness.

The Enneagram and Caring

Now, let's look at the nine different types and the lessons I have learned while caring for someone with these tendencies. The following descriptions of Enneagram types have been heavily drawn from what I have learned from two experts in the Enneagram, Ian Cron and Chuck DeGroat.[9]

The Reformer

The Reformer, type 1, is caring and has a high sense of responsibility. They have high internal standards and when they care for others, they often think of everything down to the small details. When they provide a gift as an act of caring, be assured that much thought and consideration went into the process of choosing the most perfect gift to show they care. They desire to show they care by making things around someone better and improving on things they have. At times, this desire to improve on what one has is not always well received, which can be difficult for the Reformer to understand. Reformers may take the high internal standards they have for themselves and project those high standards onto the people for whom they care.

I have found that providing care for a Reformer (also, called a Perfectionist) can be interesting. They tend to try to improve on what I have already done, which I can interpret as criticism even if it is not meant as such. Perhaps they do not want to improve on what I have done but instead offer suggestions on how they would have done it differently or better. For those who cringe at criticism, Reformers can come off as ungrateful or unappreciative, but in my experience, that is not their intention or heart's desire. Commonly, they are thankful and grateful for our care and simply cannot understand why anyone would *not* want to improve on the care they provide.

As the caregiver for a Reformer, I am learning to leave my easily offendable self at the door. It's not that I do not want to feel my feelings. When I care for someone, it is not all about me. It is about caring for them, and I find that having "thicker skin" helps me provide care without getting offended or hurt and it helps me hear their suggestions for improvement as their way of caring. Slowly, I have come to recognize that I may never meet their standards of care because their standards are out of reach or impossible for me and maybe even them. I also do not hold my breath waiting for compliments for my care; I might be holding it until my face is well past blue.

For the Reformer receiving care, it may be difficult but concentrating on what is right rather than what needs improvement may be more beneficial for the caring relationship than giving suggestions for improvement. If you need care or desire someone to care for you, consider that someone has done the best they could with what they had to offer; that is valuable. If you remember nothing else, remember the old adage: You catch more flies with honey than with vinegar. Your suggestions for improvement? Well, they may be seen as vinegar.

Are you the Reformer who desires to care for others? Reformers can have a hard time starting to care for someone because they are focused on getting everything right and perfect before they offer to care for someone. Sometimes Reformers are hesitant to even offer because they are concerned about not meeting their high standards or not being successful. My suggestion to Reformers is to not become stuck trying to perfect your care and miss the opportunities to impact someone's life. That does not mean do things haphazardly or halfhearted but be willing to provide great care even if it is not perfect. We need you to use your talents to care, and your suggestions on how to care better are important—when given at the right time.

The Helper

The Helper, or Enneagram type 2, tries to meet the needs of others and can do this out of a genuine sense of personal sacrifice. They truly like to give help and advice, and at times will give unsolicited help and advice. This can create tension as they can forget that unsolicited advice is rarely heeded or even appreciated. If they are healthy, they are thoughtful and nurturing towards others, but they can also drift towards self-deception, thinking that others are in need of more care than they actually are; are comfortable giving advice and providing care but uncomfortable asking for the same; and can at times provide care with strings attached (I cared for you, so you are obligated to care for me).

As you might imagine, caring for someone who does not feel comfortable admitting that they need care can be challenging. These are not the people that want their picture on your social media as you humblebrag about a *caring life*. Doing that creates distrust and distance and trying to care for someone you are pushing away can be difficult.

I have found that the existence of a trusting relationship with a Helper can open doors to care for them. For this reason, Helpers may be resistant to strangers caring for them. If that trusting relationship does not exist, I start building trust. Part of building trust is acknowledging the care they have provided others and sharing genuine appreciation for how they have provided care. Authenticity is important with a Helper. Although I have found that Helpers can be uncomfortable at first when being cared for, once trust is developed, a true bond can be created.

I am thankful for the Helpers in my life, and specifically my wife. If you are a Helper and desire to care for others, it is valuable to recognize that when you are healthy, you are a true blessing. Your caring heart can truly make an impact in someone's life, and I am so appreciative of the care you provide. I challenge you to consider the fact that you can only give what you have; caring for yourself or being cared for by someone else is vital. It is also valuable to consider whether your care has been requested or if you are overstepping. Since that unsolicited advice is rarely heeded, there is value to slowing down with the advice-giving unless requested. We need healthy Helpers in our uncaring world now more than ever.

If a Helper is caring for you, how should you respond to their care? Helpers love words of affirmation and appreciation. Thanking them for their care is one way they will feel appreciated. Another way is to care for them when they face a challenge, not because you feel obligated but because you are truly thankful. For those Reformers amongst us, accept the care a Helper is providing without trying to improve what they are doing. Your ideas for improvement may be valid, but most likely your ideas will be received as criticism which can be quite hurtful for a Helper.

The Achiever

The Achiever, number 3, tends to be self-confident and full of capacity. They are self-starters and passionately engage in personal growth and development to attain the goal—and the goal is success. They want to win at whatever they do and at times can blur the lines of right and wrong by focusing more on winning than how they do it. Commonly they are podcast consumers and book devourers. When it comes to caring, Achievers know how to figure out what the need is and then focus on meeting that need. They are the meal makers for the sick, and they can balance caring for multiple people at the same time. An Achiever values doing and can struggle just being present with someone who needs care.

Caring for an Achiever is hard because you need them to sit still long enough for you to have the opportunity to care for them. They can be so focused on being productive that they push aside those who are trying to care for them. Why? Because being cared for may slow them down. I have found that Achievers seem to fear slowing down because they place so much of their self-worth, consciously or unconsciously, on being a production master. They are concerned about what will happen to them if they are no longer able to produce. When it comes to caring for an Achiever, stress and its impacts are often an underlying factor. I have had many conversations with Achievers who tell me they are "not stressed at all," but once they sit still long enough to talk about what is happening in their lives the impact of stress slowly surfaces.

As a caregiver, Achievers can be some of the best of all the Enneagram types when it comes to action-oriented care, such as providing meals or helping with projects around the house. Their fear of failure and desire to perform can drive them to go over the top in trying to meet someone's needs. They do have a hard time slowing down, so caring for someone's emotional needs through presence can be outside of their comfort zone.

If you are receiving care from an Achiever, you can expect high-quality care. They will aim to provide the best care possible, though it may be hard for them to slow down and be with you. If you need someone to simply be with you during a challenging time, an Achiever might not be the best choice. Their inner anxiety to produce may leave both of you frustrated. When you thank an Achiever, focus on them as a person as much as on what they have done for you. Let them know you value them, not just what they have done.

For the Achievers receiving care, we need you to slow down a bit so we can catch up with you in order to care for you. This can be challenging and unnerving, but there are those around you who desire to care but cannot get you to sit still long enough to care for you. Learning to recognize that, although you pride yourself on being a human-machine, even machines need maintenance and care. Know that those who truly care for you are not just focused on what you do and produce but care and love who you are. When you show thanks, you do not need to go over the top and have the best thank you ever. A simple, authentic expression of gratitude will go a long way.

The Romantic

The Romantic, type 4, is one of the most unique types of people I have ever met. I wish I could be more like them when I grow up.

They do not like the ordinary and are comfortable living outside the box. Romantics are creative and self-aware. They are in touch with their feelings and thoughts and have internal freedom to express them. When it comes to caring, Romantics can pick up on someone else's emotions quickly, but they also can drift towards melancholy and read negatively into or overdramatize a caring scenario. They do not do this from a mean spirit or nefarious intentions; it is just the direction they commonly move towards. I have found Romantics to be the ones who are quick to ask the question, "How are you, *really*?" They are not content with surface responses; they are truly seeking to find out how they can care for someone.

Caring for a Romantic is always a learning experience for me. Romantics desire that their feelings be acknowledged. If you are not comfortable with your own emotions, it may be difficult to acknowledge their emotions without just wanting to move on. In the past, I have been uncomfortable with sad emotions and crying and often moved away from them quickly due to the anxiety they created in me. Romantics do not appear to sense the same anxiety from sadness, and I have had to learn to calm my inner anxieties so I can care for them where they are. Caring for a Romantic is not about fixing their difficult situation, highlighting all the good things in life, or trying to make them shrug it off and move on. It is about caring for them where they are at and walking with them towards health.

I find it refreshing to be a caregiver for a Romantic because they are often very in tune with how they are doing. They can tend to make their circumstances more severe than they truly are but walking with them and asking questions has proven valuable. Romantics will freely share how they are feeling and how they feel they are doing. This often takes the guesswork out of caring for them. I have noticed that getting beyond the presented problem to the real challenge does not take long and allows me to care for them in a way they feel cared for. I am also self-motivated to be creative in how I care for them and not settle for the routine or what I have done for someone else.

When Romantics provide care, you can expect something unique and authentic, something creative and from their heart. When Romantics provide care, they can find it perplexing when others are not as in touch with their feelings and emotions. I have also seen other Enneagram types discount Romantics' seriousness in care maybe due to their uniqueness, but Romantics provide some of the most heartfelt and authentic care. I have found that during times of grief and mourning, Romantics can care for people suffering because they are not uncomfortable with sadness.

If you are a Romantic and receiving care, you are most likely already aware that others are not as comfortable with their emotions as you are. You may need to give those providing care for you some grace if they try to cheer you up and try to move you quickly from a time of sadness. As you show appreciation to those providing care, just as it is vitally important to you, express appreciation to them for who they are and not necessarily what they are doing to care for you. Thanking them for the heart behind their care can be meaningful.

The Investigator

The Investigator, number 5, tends to be inquisitive, curious, and ingenious. They can consume and gather vast amounts of information about a multiplicity of things and then apply that information if they are ever in need of it. If I am playing *Jeopardy!*, these are the people I want on my team. When it comes to caring for others, Investigators may have a wealth of knowledge on how to care for others and might even be able to tell you how to care, but they may struggle to provide care themselves. I have found that Investigators can go through the actions of caring but they may be emotionally distant. It is not that they don't care. It is more like they are thinking through the situation and trying to make logical sense of what is happening.

Providing care for an Investigator can be interesting. I have found that an Investigator will often know a majority of the facts and details of a challenge, and in these days of Dr. Google, they have often researched and studied the ins and outs of what they are facing. There are times I have honestly been impressed by the details they know.

The demanding part of caring for Investigators is that they often want to ask a lot more questions; thus, more time must be dedicated to answering their questions. I have found they are not as satisfied with short, simple answers, and I find myself pushing my inner anxiety down so as not to create a sense of defensiveness. I tell myself, "I am not on trial." Rather, I remind myself that answering their questions in detail will help provide care in and of itself. Answers to their questions bring them an inner calmness, which makes me more than willing to do it.

As a caregiver, the Investigator is a great resource of knowledge and insight. Living and working overseas requires out-of-the-box or inventive thinking, and Investigators can have a wealth of knowledge on an issue that could work in your context and help you care for someone. When I have been in an unsettling situation or emergency, I have loved having Investigators around because they seem to grow calmer rather than amp up with emotion. They have helped me make wiser decisions in those tense moments.

A challenge that Investigators can run into is that giving of time and resources can be a barrier to caring for others. My experience is that they are gatherers of information, not necessarily givers of the information they have gathered. Through relationship building, I have seen Investigators slowly become more generous when they understand the "why" and it is not for my gain or benefit because I am caring for someone.

If you are receiving care from an Investigator, it could be awkward for both of you. Do not expect much emotion to be displayed as Investigators may seem a little uncomfortable providing care and expressing emotion. The act of caring will be there, but there might not be much visible feeling alongside it. This is not to say Investigators are insensitive. That is not true. They are sensitive. It is just that withholding of emotion and the expression of the cerebral can be part of this Enneagram type. Do not take their lack of emotional display as an offense or a slight. If you want to thank an Investigator, I have found a card or gift they can open in private works much better than a speech in front of other people.

For the Investigators, receiving care can be just as awkward as providing care. As you grow, learn to express, not withhold, your emotions from those caring for you. That can be important. Feel free to express that you prefer predictability and rhythms and to request that those providing care respect your desire for both of these. Do not forget to show your gratitude in a tangible way to those who care for you. It does not have to be public, time-consuming, or expensive. Use your inventive mind to come up with a way to show your thankfulness.

The Loyalist

The Loyalist, type 6, is faithful, dependable, reliable, and accountable. Loyalists are courageous but can drift towards worry, which is driven by an inner sense of fear of the unknown. They can spend considerable amounts of time planning for possibilities even if they are improbable, and they can spend time thinking about worst-case scenarios that may never come to fruition. They find comfort in the fact that they have thought about it and how they would respond if it did happen. When it comes to caring for others, Loyalists are quick to be concerned for others and often are the first ones to reach out to see how others are doing. They don't like the feeling of being left behind, so they will try to make sure others are not left behind. They are all about preventative care and seek to help others so they can avoid needing reactive care.

It is important to note that when caring for a Loyalist, although they may put on a courageous front, they often have internal fears and anxieties driving their actions. When caring for them, it is important to remember that they value reliability and predictability. They commonly place these as high priorities and assume others do also. They do not like sudden changes and can seem disheveled for a few days when a big change has taken place. Needing care is often a big change for a Loyalist. I have found that once a Loyalist admits and accepts care, they will most often not forget. They are not quick to move on or move past; as their name states, they will become loyal to you for what you have done for them during their time of need.

As a caregiver, the Loyalist can be compassionate and empathetic. At times, they will worry more about you and your challenge than you do. Although this may seem harmless at the outset, in the long term it is not healthy. As I mentioned, Loyalists like to think about different scenarios and at times can forget that thinking about caring for someone and actually caring for them are not the same thing. But if you are fortunate to have a Loyalist as a caregiver, you will experience someone who can provide consistency and stability and will consider caring for you as an honor and a privilege.

If you are a Loyalist receiving care, it can be uncomfortable for you, specifically if it is a spontaneous thing. It is your nature to be kind and appreciative *if* you were planning on something, but if you were not planning on it, you may react rather than respond. Remember to not only think about sharing your thankfulness for the care you are receiving but verbalize and express your gratitude. You may worry about how those providing care for you are being impacted. I encourage you to share your concern, but if you can fight the tendency to use internal worry and fear to block others from caring for you, it will be to your advantage.

The Enthusiast

The Enthusiast, Enneagram number 7, tends to love excitement, happiness, and spontaneity. They enjoy flexibility and are optimists. They have the innate ability to captivate a room with their storytelling and imagination. In general, they do not shy away from being the center of attention. When it comes to caring, Enthusiasts can bring joy to those who are suffering and can care for those who are struggling as they move through a difficult time. The lack of desire to stay in one place or remain focused for a long time can be a barrier for Enthusiasts. They may have the focus to care when something is new and just unfolding, but if care turns into a longer-term situation, they can quickly lose focus and move on to something else.

Providing care for an Enthusiast can be challenging in that they are not interested in feeling emotions like sadness and hurt. They tend to focus on being glad. Rather than feel sadness and hurt, they can reframe or refocus on a positive or alternative perspective of what they are facing. Because Enthusiasts love variety and spontaneity, a caregiver may need to adapt their care with more flexibility. It may also be difficult for the caregiver to initially move beyond the superficial, specifically if the real challenge does not promote feelings of gladness and joy. In my experience as a caregiver, I am not looking to sit down and process difficult emotions. Do not get offended if the Enthusiast does not want to do this.

As a caregiver, the Enthusiast is one of the best Enneagram types that I like to be around if I am feeling down and desire to see a different perspective. They can add variety to life and help you see your situation from a more positive perspective. It may be a challenge for them to stick with you through a long illness or a more extended challenging time. It is not impossible, but their tendency to move to something new and exciting could be a barrier too difficult to push through.

If you are an Enthusiast receiving care, it is valuable to recognize that not everyone is able to be as flexible and spontaneous as you are. Other Enneagram types are planners and perfectionists, so the care they can provide might put a damper on your desire for something new and exciting. One possible way to use your innate gifting and pursuit for fun and excitement is in how you show gratitude to those caring for you. It may be a stretch for them, but the joy you bring to a room can be refreshing and recharging for caregivers.

The Challenger

The Challenger, or the 8 on the Enneagram, is known for tendencies of self-confidence, aggressiveness, and independence. The Challenger is self-motivated, driven, and laser focused. They commonly have new ideas and see potential opportunities all around them. When it comes to caring, they desire to protect and defend those being mistreated and will come quickly to the aid of someone in a difficult situation. My experience with Challengers is that they like to demonstrate control even when it comes to caring for others.

Providing care for a Challenger can be a slow march. The Challengers in my life do not like to show vulnerability or weakness. They are used to defending and caring for others, so when it comes to admitting or showing they need care, it can be difficult. In my experience, a Challenger struggles with expressing that they need care because it goes directly against their internal instinct of showing strength and control. I have also found that Challengers have a select few people in their life that they trust, and in the right setting where they feel safe, they will open up about needing care or what weighs heavy on their heart. Letting their guard down is not an everyday or weekly occurrence, but when they let it down and let someone in, count it an honor.

As a caregiver for a Challenger, I have learned to be patient. The Challenger has a fear of being betrayed, taken advantage of, or being exploited for their vulnerability. With that in mind, I realize for them to reach out for care or to accept it takes courage and strength. I have learned to follow their lead and go at their pace. When I have tried to do otherwise, the defense mechanisms and walls go up quickly. The issue of confidence and privacy is paramount for all Enneagram types, but it is accentuated with a Challenger. They do not want their stories shared with others, and if they want them shared, they will do it themselves. The quickest way to block the ability to care for a Challenger is to share a challenge they are facing with another and have them hear that you have been sharing their story.

I have seen Challengers care for those who are being mistreated or taken advantage of time and time again. A healthy Challenger has little to no tolerance for people hurting other people. They do not struggle with any hesitation to act and do not normally take long to decide to care. If you are looking for someone to take the lead on a care plan, they will make it happen.

A barrier that Challengers can struggle with when they provide care is opening up to the person receiving care. Letting their guard down and sharing about times they were weak and in need of care can be difficult because they can confuse vulnerability and transparency with weakness. But on the flip side, if they are unable to share their humanness and vulnerability, it is hard for others to identify with them; it can make other Enneagram types wary of receiving their care. If Challengers are going to be vulnerable while providing care, it needs to be authentic.

If you are a Challenger receiving care, I know it can feel risky to accept care from others. And honestly, accepting care can be a risky thing. But if you resist being cared for and follow the narrative that you are self-reliant and self-sufficient, it will be hard for those in your life to identify with you. I have witnessed that, over time, others will quit trying to care for you; they will move on to someone who is easier to love and care for. One last thing, when someone is caring for you, softening the command-and-control communication style is important for the caregiver. You may be used to giving orders and telling others what to do, but when you are receiving care, softening your tone can go a long way in showing appreciation and expressing trust to those who care for you.

The Peacemaker

The Peacemaker, number 9, is the one who has the tendency and abilities to know how to relax and go with the flow of things. They are the people I want around on vacation or when I am looking to have a fun time. Peacemakers, as the name suggests, commonly avoid conflict. When it comes to caring, they are some of the most generous people you will ever meet. They hold possessions loosely and will sacrifice to care for someone else even if it means they will suffer because of it. They commonly, and without hesitation, put others ahead of themselves. I have several people in my life who are Peacemakers, and I am very thankful for them.

When it comes to caring for Peacemakers, I have found they are some of the easiest people to care for in the sense that they will, on the surface, accept almost anything you do for them and will be thankful. But I also find them to be some of the hardest people to understand or discern if I am truly and effectively caring for them. Unlike some Enneagram types that are quick to offer suggestions on care and how you can better care for them, Peacemakers want to avoid any semblance of conflict and will accept care even if it is not meeting their needs.

As the caregiver for a Peacemaker, I observe how they provide care for others and use this as a clue on how they may like to be cared for. It is not always accurate, but it gives me a good place to begin. If I don't know their preferences, I ask them. However, I have found their response to my question about their preferences depends on their trust in our relationship. If the trust is high, they will share honestly with me. But sometimes they may not be open to the idea of sharing openly. In this case, I have learned that if I am patient, eventually they will share how they like to be cared for. If I am still not making headway by asking or observing, I have found I can offer a few options of how I could care for them that might help them express their desires.

For Peacemakers caring for others, making decisions related to caring for others can be one of the first barriers. You have a generous heart and a caring soul but making decisions on specifics can block you from putting your thoughts and ideas into action. Then, once you put your caring thoughts into action, caring for yourself while caring for others and not being taken advantage of is paramount. Having a trusted friend that can speak the truth to you about what they observe in your life can be invaluable.

If you are a Peacemaker receiving care, those around you who are healthy, whole, and trustworthy desire to truly care for you. If asked, it can be valuable to share how you best prefer to be cared for so that the caregiver can more effectively care for you. It can be uncomfortable and uneasy to do this, but if you can share how you truly desire to be cared for, it will be less conflictive for both you and the caregiver. Very few people want to care for someone in a way they do not feel cared for, and if the ones caring for you are healthy, whole, and trustworthy, they will be able to hear your true thoughts without offense.

DEVELOPING YOUR CARING LIFE

The Enneagram can be a valuable tool to help you and me care for others. Understanding our individual tendencies and the tendencies of the Enneagram types can help us see how we can provide the best care possible. The following questions will help you as you grow in your understanding of the Enneagram and your *caring life*:

The Reformer

1. Do you have a Reformer in your life that you care for?

2. What are challenges you face in caring for them?

3. How does understanding the tendencies of a Reformer help you better care for them?

The Helper

1. Do you enjoy caring for those with Helper tendencies?

2. What are some things that make Helpers easy or difficult to care for?

3. How does understanding the tendencies of a Helper help you better care for them?

The Achiever

1. What are your experiences caring for those with Achiever tendencies?

2. If you are an Achiever, do the descriptions in the chapter describe how you feel cared for? What are some reasons you agree or disagree?

3. As an Achiever, what type of person do you like to care for? Which is easier? Which is more difficult?

The Romantic

1. Do you have any Romantics in your life that you care for?

2. What are a few things you wish Romantics understood about being on the other side of caring for them?

3. How does understanding the tendencies of a Romantic help you better care for them?

The Investigator

1. Do you enjoy caring for those with Investigator tendencies?

2. What are some things that make Investigators easy or difficult to care for?

3. How does understanding the tendencies of Investigators help you better care for them? Are there things you will change?

The Loyalist

1. What are your experiences caring for those with Loyalist tendencies?

2. If you are a Loyalist, do the descriptions in the chapter describe how you feel cared for? What are some reasons you agree or disagree?

3. As a Loyalist, what type of person do you like to care for? Which is easier? Which is more difficult?

The Enthusiast

1. Do you have any Enthusiasts in your life that you care for?

2. What are a few things you wish Enthusiasts understood about what it is like being on the other side of caring for them?

3. As an Enthusiast, what type of person do you like to care for? Which is easier? Which is more difficult?

The Challenger

1. Are you drawn to care for those with Challenger tendencies? If so, what are some reasons for this?

2. Can you describe an experience caring for a Challenger? How did you feel during and after caring for them?

3. How does understanding the tendencies of a Challenger help you better care for them? Are there things you will change?

The Peacemaker

1. What are your experiences caring for those with Peacemaker tendencies?

2. If you are a Peacemaker, do the descriptions in the chapter describe how you feel cared for? What are some reasons you agree or disagree?

3. As a Peacemaker, what type of person do you like to care for? Which is easier? Which is more difficult?

CHAPTER 5

Expectations and Assumptions in Caring

G oing to the rural areas to provide care was one of the high-lights of my almost 14 years living and serving in Mad-agascar. There was always unexpected adventure. Inevitably I forgot to bring something with me or brought something with me that should have been left at home. Once I flew to a rural area with all the car and house keys and did not realize it until I landed. My wife Heather had no way of getting into the house or using a car. (A big thank you to Jay and Nate who came to the rescue!)

One thing I enjoyed about traveling to rural areas was that I saw the impact of the care we provided. The villagers were very appreciative. I had the opportunity to care for people as they battled conditions that most people will never see or will only read about in textbooks.

The people in these villages were suffering due to the lack of access to care that is standard in the developed world, and often-times they were manipulated by ancestral worship practices that left them in fear of seeking care outside their village. Still, once their possessions were gone and the witch doctor had taken everything he or she could from them, they showed up in a clinic.

We returned to one village month after month, and we noticed we were providing care for intestinal problems and a disease called *schistosomiasis*, both of which are commonly related to unclean water.

If you like interesting diseases or the show *Monsters Inside Me*, schistosomiasis is right up your alley. The parasite penetrates the skin of someone wading, bathing, or swimming and migrates to the bladder or intestines. Eventually, the person will have blood in either their urine or stool. Further down the road when the liver is impacted, their belly swells to the size of a pregnant woman's. The treatment is simple but can be harsh—ingesting poison to kill the living parasite inside the body.

We were giving out the treatment for this like it was candy. Everyone seemed to have the same problem on repeat. I am all about prevention, so we began to ask more questions and dig into what the villagers thought the problem was. What could be some of the reasons they were continually sick? There were many varying ideas and thoughts.

Eventually, we reached a discussion on the source of their drinking water. We asked if we could see where their drinking water came from. I was interested to know about the source for two reasons: (1) our little investigation and (2) my self-preservation. This water source was surely where the water was drawn to prepare our food.

When we arrived at the creek, it was evident that the water source was not the cleanest: There were cows in the water drinking; people bathing; dishes being washed; clothes being laundered; people brushing their teeth; *and* people drawing water into buckets for drinking. This was all taking place in about a 30-meter stretch of very slow-moving water.

In my mind, the solution became clear. From our perspective, we saw that they needed a well. They needed a clean source of drinking water so that they were not using the same water for all their needs. We began to gather funds, look for someone who could dig a well, and make other preparations, but before breaking ground, we needed to discuss how the well was to be used and who would use it. The village chief shared that they were so excited to have a well for the cows to drink from. I was not expecting to hear that. Clean water for the cows? What about the people? He told us the cows could drink the water, but the people had to bathe and drink the water their ancestors had used. If not, they would insult the ancestors.

Incorrect Analysis

In their book *Noise*, Daniel Kahneman, Olivier Sibony, and Cass Sunstein articulated this conundrum eloquently. They discuss that "most of us, most of the time, live with the unquestioned belief that the world looks as it does because that is the way it is."[10] The way I see the world is the way it is. The next critical assumption is that other people view the world the way I do. With these assumptions, we invest very little time or energy, if any, in listening, observing, and considering whether there are alternative ways of seeing what we see.

Social psychologists know this line and pattern of thought as *naïve realism*. The way I see the world is the commonsense way of seeing the world. Directly or indirectly, we make the judgment that if you do not see it the way I see it, you must be uninformed, irrational, or inexperienced.

I believe the majority of people are considerate and wise. They do what they do, care the way they do, think the way they think, and talk the way they talk because they think it is the right way to do it. I have not met many people in my 44 years on this planet that wake up in the morning with the idea that they will do it this way because it is the wrong way to think, act, care, or talk. We think our way is the best. The obvious way. The most practical way. The easiest. The fastest. The cheapest. The most honorable. The most ideal. Substitute whatever word you want in there.

Imagine (or maybe you do not need to because you have practical experience) how these assumptions and linked expectations can impact how we care for people. If we believe that others want to be cared for the way we want to be cared for, then that is what we do and that is how we care for them. I want someone to come and visit me in the hospital, so I will visit them in the hospital. I want someone to fix me a meal, so I will fix them a meal. I want someone to call me on the phone rather than send a text, so I will call them on the phone rather than send a text.

This extends to how others will receive and respond to the care I give: *Obviously, they will receive my care the way I would, and they will respond to my care the way I would because the way I care and respond is the "right" way to do it.* We may not verbalize this, but I guarantee it is there subconsciously. *They will write a thank you card because obviously that is what you do for someone who provides you a meal when you are sick. They will compliment you in front of friends and family for the help you gave them. That is the obvious thing to do. They will create a nice post on Facebook thanking me for all to see. Again, that is clearly what you do. They will call you and thank you when you send a financial gift to help their mounting medical bills. It is so obvious.*

But here is the truth: If we want to be intentional in how we care for others, then we must learn how *they* desire to be cared for. The best time to learn this is before you care for them. Wiser people than I have noticed that one of the biggest keys to knowing how someone desires to be cared for is to observe how they care for others. To know this, we must listen, observe, and notice how they respond to life challenges in other people's lives. It might not be right all the time, but it is a great place to start.

Admitting that maybe, just maybe, the way I give and receive care might not be the only and right way is a constant battle. The idea seems simplistic and evident, but if we are not vigilant, we will drift back to the way we do things and the way we want things done for us. It is easier. It takes less time and energy. It takes less mental space and less intentionality. But the results are far from the same.

Dr. Gary Chapman's study of the five love languages is primarily for marriage and family, but it is also applicable for how we care for people in general. For those not familiar with Dr. Chapman and his book *The Five Love Languages*, he talks about five different love languages: words of affirmation, acts of service, receiving gifts, quality time, and physical touch. He shares that knowing our love language preferences and the preferences of those we love and care for helps decrease conflict and increase connection.[11]

My wife Heather and I were introduced to *The Five Love Languages* when we went through marriage counseling. We were able to identify each other's preferences, which has decreased conflict and helped us build a stronger marriage, but I still find myself trying to love and care for my wife the way in which I prefer to be cared for. If I do this for the person I love the most, I guarantee I drift in how I care for others.

For example, I am a big fan of apple pie. Not just any apple pie though. It has to be homemade apple pie. Keep those store-bought ones with more syrup and sugar than apples. Sign me up for the homemade apple pie. Anytime. Any day. Homemade apple pies are the fast lane to my heart.

Early in our marriage, Heather and I were at her parents' house, and Heather made some apple pies. I patiently waited until after dinner to have my favorite part of the meal. My father-in-law and I cut the pie, and I must admit I like big pieces of pie, so I prefer to cut my own.

I asked Heather if she wanted milk with her pie. She responded that she did. I got the milk from the fridge and began to pour it on her piece of pie. In my family, "milk with your pie" means your pie is swimming in milk. My father-in-law looked perplexed, but for me, I was doing my best to care for my wife in preparing her pie the way I wanted my pie prepared. When I gave Heather the pie, she was not pleased. She asked: "Are you joking?" I was not. It was a miss. A genuine attempt, but a miss, nonetheless.

Obviously, this can easily happen in situations much more vital and impactful than apple pie, but you get the point. Learning someone's love language and learning to ask for clarification can go a long way in helping your efforts have the impact you desire.[12]

Before we go further, you may be wondering how the love language of physical touch plays into caring for others. Perhaps you are thinking, "I'm OK with all of those except physical touch, specifically when it comes to caring for someone outside my marriage and close family." I understand. For the nurses and those trained in therapeutic touch who are reading this, know that caring touch has great value. Unfortunately, our over-sexualized world has turned a caring touch into something it was never intended to be, so my suggestion is that unless you have a working understanding and training in the ethics of appropriate, caring physical touch, do not practice it.

Expectations

Peter Scazzero's work in *Emotional Healthy Spirituality* has been transformational for many, myself included. Scazzero cites Pat Ennis on this topic of expectations and how, if we are not intentional, they hinder, hamper, and at times destroy relationships. His discussion on expectations is tucked back in chapter nine of his book.[13] I tend to fade as I reach the end of a book, and I missed it the first two times I read it. My friend Zach brought it back to my attention, and I began to zero in on it.

More than any other page in any other book I have read in the last 10 years (excluding the Bible), Scazzero's two pages on expectations absolutely transformed how I provide and receive care. They are pages I frequently return to. Clarifying our expectations and the expectations of those we provide care for is invaluable.

Scazzero discusses four main types of expectations: unconscious, unspoken, not-agreed-upon, and unrealistic. Let's look at each of those along with a practical example about how each may unfold as we care for others.

Unconscious Expectations

Unconscious expectations are the expectations deeply embedded in our thought processes. Most of the time we are not aware of these expectations until something unfolds. When a situation or interaction unfolds and our unconscious expectations are not realized, we can become irritated, frustrated, angry, and agitated. These emotions arise from the fact that the situation did not turn out the way our unconscious mind thought it would. As someone who provides care, I know this can happen very easily and can be very painful.

I grew up in church. I have been around the church my whole life. I have seen how unconscious expectations, if not recognized, can be detrimental. For example, maybe someone in the church is sick and has been unable to leave the house for several days. You hear about this and volunteer to pick up groceries and anything else they need from the store. The church member is grateful, gives you the list, and volunteers to reimburse you for the expenditures. You respond by saying that you can settle the costs when you get to their house.

After visiting several different stores around town, you find all the necessary things the church member has requested. You knock on the door. It is unlocked, so you unload the car and bring the groceries into the house. You call for the person and they call back that the money for the groceries is on the counter and thank you for helping them in a time of need.

As you leave the house, you find yourself irritated, agitated, and on edge. As you think about some reasons for these feelings, they seem to center around the fact that your friend never came to the door. You never saw his face. You think it would have been the kind and respectful thing to come to the door and thank you face to face for your help. That is what you would have done. You would never treat someone helping you like this.

See how unconscious expectations can begin to spiral in a situation like this one? Scazzero shares that the way to prevent unconscious expectations from causing hurt is to think, ponder, and consider what expectations we have for others as we provide care. If the someone you are caring for is someone you trust, it is valuable to have a discussion with them about expectations. When you consider your expectations before something happens, you have the opportunity to respond, not only react.

Regi Campbell writes that when we react, we normally only use our heart. Reaction is full of emotion. Our emotions come from God. I am not saying that our emotions are a bad or negative thing, but I certainly have some life experiences that I would like a redo on, to respond rather than react. When it comes to unconscious expectations, I drift towards reacting rather than responding. Responding involves using both my head and my heart, not divorcing one from the other. When we can respond to a situation rather than react, Campbell shares, we bring strategy to our energy.[14]

If you feel irritated and agitated after caring for someone, take the time to ask yourself why you feel the way you feel. If you do not, it becomes very easy to project your emotions onto the person you are caring for. We cannot hold someone responsible to meet expectations that we only became aware of after the situation unfolded. Though many times we do just that.

If we then carry those feelings and unrealized expectations into other relationships, we end up hurting those closest to us. What can we do? I have found that if I am patient, pausing and considering the situation is a valuable step. I ask God to reveal reasons why my act of caring has left me frustrated and ask Him to help uncover some of my unconscious expectations.

Unspoken Expectations

Unspoken expectations are similar to unconscious ones, but they are clarified as expectations that we *are* conscious of and have thought about but have not shared with another person. They are different than unconscious ones because we are aware of them before and while we are caring for someone, but we have not expressed them. So, even though we have not shared or voiced our expectations, we are irritated, frustrated, and disappointed when the person we are caring for or who is caring for us does not meet our expectations. Or we have these same feelings of frustration and disappointment when the person caring for us does not respond the way we want them to, again, even though we did not give them a hint or the courtesy of sharing what we desire from them.

Keeping with the example of picking up groceries, let's look at it from the perspective of unspoken expectations. This time a family member has not been feeling well. You know they cannot leave the house, so you volunteer to get the groceries for them. They are so appreciative and thank you for your kindness when you deliver their groceries. They reimburse you for the groceries and give you extra money for the gas because you drove around town finding all the special health foods they eat. You are glad you are able to help.

The family member recovers from their sickness. The next time you are together as a family is on Thanksgiving. Before dinner, the family member personally thanks you again for what you did. Now, your family has a tradition of sharing what each person is thankful for before eating. Normally, you would rather go straight to the eating part, but this year you are interested in the thanksgiving because you have done so much for them and you are sure they will share how thankful they are for you and what you have done. However, your unspoken expectations of your family member are not to be realized.

Instead, when your family member shares the one thing they are thankful for, they share about how your cousin came and mowed the grass for them while they were sick and how he took their dog out for long walks so their favorite Shih Tzu could get some exercise. They were so thankful for your cousin and his thoughtfulness. You feel your face growing red and you squirm in your seat. They failed to mention you and what you had done. If they were truly thankful for what you had done, they would have thanked you publicly in front of the family like they thanked your cousin.

When it comes to expectations and judgments, it is often that two-letter word *if* that can cause us major heartache. In my experience, when I begin to use *if*, it signifies to me that I am expecting someone to act or behave in a way of my choosing. When they do not act in the way I want them to, I insert the *if*, a small word that causes many hurts due to the judgments and expectations we place on others.

Not-Agreed-Upon Expectations

Geri Scazzero, Peter's wife, was the first person I heard share about not-agreed-upon expectations. She said that expectations are only valid if both parties or people have agreed to them. If not, they remain wishes, hopes, and desires but are not valid expectations. When I think about the frustrations I have had when I cared for people, most of them fall into this category. I had a lot of wishes, but I did not give the other person the opportunity to share their perspective on my expectations or to choose whether to agree or disagree with them.

I commonly share with patients that I am not a prophet, and I am not able to predict what they want or what will happen. I need them to tell me or at least give me some pretty strong clues.

Even still, that is exactly what I expect of others when it comes to me. I whimsically want prophets and prophetesses who know my expectations and agree on them, even if we have never discussed and agreed on them.

Let's return to the groceries scenario, but this time we are caring for a coworker. You have worked with this person for several years and you have a great working relationship. You hear they are sick, so you volunteer to pick some things up for them so they do not have to venture out while feeling unwell. You talk to your coworker about what she will need. She is so thankful and agrees to pay for the groceries. You mention that you are glad to get them and will use your pickup truck, which uses a lot of gas. You kindly request that she reimburse you for the gas.

You run around town in your truck and find the groceries she requested. When you arrive at her house, you unload the groceries and see your coworker who does not look well. She gladly reimburses you for the cost of the groceries, gives you a thank you card with a gift card in it, and expresses her gratefulness for what you have done to help her.

You wait awkwardly for the gas money, but she does not bring it up, and as you leave her house, you think, "She is a cheapskate." She gave you the money for the groceries, but she did not offer a dime for the gas you used running all over town for her gluten-free, specialty health foods. You mentioned the truck and gas money to her. You expected her to be a little more considerate and give you money for the fuel. You gladly volunteered your time, but why would she be so disrespectful and not give you the money for the gas?

In this situation, you had expectations of the fuel being reimbursed, and you voiced that expectation, but it was not actually agreed upon. She probably would have given you the gas money if you had agreed upon it, or maybe because she was sick, she truly forgot. She did not agree to your expectation, yet you want to hold her accountable for something she did not agree to.

When she returns to work, she shares with your colleagues how you helped her out in her time of need. She shares with several coworkers that you are a truly caring friend. Your coworkers thank you for being so kind to her and caring for her, but all you can think is that she is cheap and using flattery to cover it up. You wanted your gas money, not pleasantries.

Unrealistic Expectations

Unrealistic expectations are expectations we place on someone else that are impossible for them to meet. In general, unrealistic expectations come from a place of self-focus rather than mutual focus. But just like unconscious, unspoken, and not-agreed-upon expectations can impact care, unrealistic expectations also have the high potential to create relational tension and hurt.

For instance, you become aware that your pastor is sick and not doing well. You have the idea to organize meals for her and her family. The last time someone did this for you, you ended up eating lasagna 10 days in a row. You organize a meal train, so she and her family receive a variety of meals. The pastor is so thankful. She sends you a thank you card and a gift card to your favorite restaurant. But what you *really* want is to be the pastor's best friend and confidant and for her to be available to help you any time you are in need.

In the process of organizing and caring for the pastor, you become sick yourself. You are sure she will return the favor and do the same as you have done for her. She is not yet fully recovered from her illness, but that is no excuse. Your caring deserves an equal or better response.

As we read this scenario, it is evident that the expectations in this case are unrealistic. It is easy to pick out the unrealistic expectations here, especially when it is someone else's unrealistic expectations. Yet, when I am in the middle of the scene, my objectivity goes out the window. Subjectivity rules the day. I react and judge rather than respond. Placing unrealistic expectations on others is harmful to both you and them.

Assumptions

Assumptions and expectations are similar. Assumptions are things I assume are true. Some assumptions are that everyone loves West Virginia Mountaineer football, everyone loves trout fishing, and everyone loves eating homemade apple pie.

I imagine you have a story (or stories!) of when you assumed something was true only to find out that it was not. Sometimes those assumptions can lead to incorrect conclusions about who, what, when, where, and why. These five things are super important, and even being off on one of them can have a major impact.

Assumptions include what you think another person knows about a certain situation or someone else's story. When caring for others, it is paramount to consider our assumptions. In our house, we are fans of the phrase "it is not my story to tell," meaning that we do not have the right to share another's story, whether positive, negative, or somewhere in between, unless that person gave express permission to do so and said *exactly* what can be shared. Sometimes when we care for oth- ers, we "assume" we can share their story, only to find out theydid not want their story shared with others.

Another important thing in the area of assumptions is when we bring our perspective, knowledge, and experience into the caring opportunity, we can assume that what is common knowledge and evident to us is also common knowledge and evident to the one we are caring for.

∨

We must learn how others desire to be cared for.

In many areas these assumptions can be navigated and worked out. One tricky area is trust. Assuming levels of trust can make things challenging. Sometimes we assume that the one we are caring for trusts us at the same level we trust, only to find out that our trust levels are vastly different.

I remember one of my first medical clinics in the bush. Normally, when working in a clinic, we were either in the mobile clinic or under a tree. This particular day was *super* hot, and we were sitting under a nice big shade tree. I sat down to treat patients, and I was amazed that most of the complaints were the same: blood in their urine. I heard it over and over again, and we shared with each one that the cause of this was from the water they used for bathing, though I am not sure they were convinced we knew what we were talking about. Having a common problem makes diagnosing a lot easier: same medicine, same treatment, same education, same follow-up.

One lady waited for hours, saying she wanted to go last. She had brought her son to see us but did not want the others to know what his problem was. She told us that when her son peed the urine was yellow. She knew there must be something wrong with him or why would his urine be this color. She assumed that her son was the sick one, not all the others who were urinating blood. Her assumption was wrong. Our perspective can shape our assumptions.

It is the same with assumptions as with expectations. Clarification and questions are the best way to proceed when caring for someone. Questions like: What are some unconscious expectations I may have in caring for my friend? What is my plan to communicate my expectations kindly and respectfully? When do I plan on discussing my expectations so that we can agree on both sets of expectations? What are some unrealistic expectations that I might have? Who do I trust to tell me the truth in love and help me process my expectations to decide if they are realistic or not? What are some assumptions I have about the person I am caring for and how they will receive my care?

It takes time to go through this process, and at times the process can be cumbersome, but I have never regretted asking more questions than fewer questions or seeking clarification. Most importantly, going through this process will decrease your frustrations and the frustrations of the person you are caring for.

DEVELOPING YOUR CARING LIFE

Incorrect analysis, expectations, and assumptions all impact our *caring life*. If we can be more aware of them and develop a plan to address them, the care we provide will be impacted in a positive way. Seeking clarity and personal application in our analysis, expectations, and assumptions is paramount. The following questions will help you reflect on how you can grow personally in these three areas:

Incorrect Analysis

1. How do your desires to be cared for impact how you care for others?

2. How can you integrate the five love languages into how you care for others?

3. What is one of the biggest challenges you have in caring for someone in their love language, and how can you overcome it?

Expectations

1. Have you ever experienced unspoken expectations when caring for someone? What were those unspoken expectations?

2. Do you find it difficult to share your expectations? What are some reasons it is difficult for you to share them?

3. What is realistic and unrealistic can be subjective. How can you navigate this subjectivity when caring for others?

4. How would you approach a conversation so that expectations can be agreed upon?

Assumptions

1. Can you remember a time when you assumed something that ended up not being true? How did you feel?

2. What are some common assumptions in caring that you have experienced?

3. Have you seen assumptions create tension in you and in those you have cared for? What is your plan to avoid making assumptions going forward?

CHAPTER 6

The Who, What, When, How, and Why of Communicating Care

I n the last 20 years, my family has traveled back and forth across the ocean a lot, much of it done separately—either I go ahead of the family or Heather and the kids go ahead of me to whichever country we are traveling to. Our kids are great travelers, and my wife Heather is a champ for having traveled with toddlers on long flights alone.

One summer, I returned to Madagascar a week ahead of my family to host American visitors for a Madagascar church conference. On the night I was to meet my family at the airport, I was still struggling with jetlag. (I am about as good of friends with jetlag as I am with calculus; we tolerate each other but are glad to part ways when the time comes.) I planned to lay down for a quick nap and then pick my family up later that night.

That evening I succumbed to jetlag and my short nap became a long one. I did not wake up as planned. I scurried out of bed, jumped into our STL Land Cruiser,[15] and groggily drove towards the airport to meet my family.

Halfway to the airport, I received a message from my wife that said, "Do NOT come to the airport." This was beginning to feel like a bad dream. I am known for my sleepwalking expeditions. In fact, I have run out of the house and tried to break into someone else's home while sleepwalking. But I had never driven a car in such a state. Was I driving the car in a sleepwalking dream? Fortunately, and unfortunately, I was awake.

I began to wonder why Heather was telling me not to come to the airport. Had I overslept so much that I missed picking them up, and they found another ride home? Not the best demonstration of a loving husband and father. But as I was soon to find out, my oversleeping was a best-case scenario.

As I remember it, I was approaching the airport and looked up in the sky just beyond the runway. I saw a plane struggling and heard the roars of the engines. I have been on small planes in the bush that required similar maneuvers whenever a cow or goat ran onto a grass runway, but it did not appear that this plane was made for quick directional changes.

As I watched the plane shaking and seemingly struggle to gain altitude, I received another message from Heather: "I Love You." That was it. The plane disappeared into the night sky. No other messages. Nothing. I made my way into the airport to ask about what happened. Inside was mass chaos. No one seemed to know what was going on, or if they did know, they were not telling me. So, I turned around and went home. It was surreal. I was supposed to be returning home with my family.

Steve Cuss has helped me learn that when I get anxious, I go into action mode.[16] I cannot sit still. I need to do something, not because my actions are valuable, but because they calm my inner anxiety. This night was no different. I was super anxious. I called the airline, which is known for many things except good customer service. I had high hopes that in a situation like this, they would be more helpful and caring. I explained the situation to the customer service agent on the other end of the line, and she coldly responded: "I cannot confirm or deny the location of the aircraft in question." That was it. No further explanation. Silence on her end. I nervously laughed thinking that certainly she could do better than this.

I explained again that my wife and kids were on that plane and I needed to know where they were. Surely we were just experiencing a language barrier thing (i.e., my French) or a bad cell connection. Because she could not really have just said, "I cannot confirm or deny the location of the aircraft in question," knowing my wife and kids were on the plane. So, like a good American, when you do not communicate well the first time, you try again…only louder, right? I asked again a little louder but still kind, holding out hope that she did not hear me or did not understand my French. The response was the same: "I cannot confirm or deny the location of the aircraft in question."

To put my conversation and anxiety into perspective, this was several months after Malaysian flight 370 disappeared into the Indian Ocean. If you remember that crash, it consumed the news cycle for quite some time, specifically in Madagascar and the Indian Ocean basin as the aviation authorities searched for the plane. My mind quickly went where no husband or parent wants to go. My whole life was on that plane, and the lady I was speaking with could not or chose not to confirm or deny the location of the aircraft they were on. For all I knew, they were somewhere in the Indian Ocean like the Malaysian flight.

I know the agent I spoke with may not have been able to give me all the answers I wanted or thought I needed at the time, but I have no doubt she could have communicated in a more caring manner. The whole experience made me reflect on how import-

Concentrate on the basics of communication— the who, what, when, how, and why.

ant it is to communicate with a caring attitude and voice in those times that people are in need of care.

Communication can get complicated and can appear complex. There are so many mediums to communicate that you care, so how do you choose which one to use and when to use it, and how do you know if your care is effectively communicated? It is hard to know at times what you are communicating and why, and maybe you feel like you do not have the time and resources to communicate effectively. I have found that concentrating on the basics of communication—the who, what, when, how, and why—helps me as I communicate my care to others.

Starting with the Why

It is valuable to begin with the "why" or the reason behind focusing on communication in care.

I am a person who likes to plan far in advance. I love to have a plan and spend hours and days of my life coming up with plans or pathways on how to care more efficiently and effectively for other people. One trap that I can easily fall into is "me think."

Me think is when I get so engrossed in a plan or project that it becomes very clear in my mind. I pray, develop a plan, discuss it, research it, and then act on it. The plan is clear to me because I have spent so much time thinking about it. But it is not as clear to others. In fact, at times my ideas and plans, although good and valuable, created hurt and confusion because I failed to communicate, and by not communicating, I communicated to others that they do not belong or matter.

My conclusion: I must put as much time into communicating my thoughts and plans as I do in developing them. This is so necessary when it comes to caring for others. I can devise a great plan and have all the details laid out but then put a rush on it to get it into action and drop the ball on communication, and then in the process, I make a challenging time for someone more challenging due to my lack of clear communication or ineffective communication. That increases instability rather than provides stability. It increases inconsistency rather than consistency, and instability and inconsistency are two of the last things someone needs when walking through turbulent times.

The airline representative I spoke with was following a plan the airline had in place for just such an emergency or crisis. I now understand that countless hours go into developing plans for crises such as I experienced. During one of those meetings a decision was made to not tell families information about a flight emergency until they had all the official details.

The reason for not giving details of an emergency was clear to all involved, but they failed to communicate the reasons to people (like me!) who were asking for information and looking for a caring voice in the middle of a crisis. The "why" or importance of communicating care was probably not included in the airline's plan, and therefore, I perceived her communication as uncaring and that my family was not important enough for them to give me the information I sought.

The What of Communicating Care

Before exploring the specifics and practical tips, it will be valuable to first examine two human needs that come into play when we communicate care. Executive business coach and author Dr. Chip Dodd has taught me so much concerning human emotions and needs, and specifically the importance of *belonging* and *mattering*. Through his books and podcasts, but mostly in conversations, Chip has helped me understand how our needs and emotions are not weaknesses to be suppressed or denied; rather, our needs and emotions are the way we were created and they help us connect.

In his book *The Needs of the Heart*, Chip describes the two most basic human needs as belonging and mattering.[17] Belonging, he notes, is being accepted for who we are as spiritual and emotional beings. Belonging is having the trust and freedom to be human with someone else. This provides us with the knowledge that there is somewhere we are welcomed, accepted, and known.

My friend and author Dick Foth adds that these belonging relationships are built through chemistry over time or under pressure.[18] When someone is in need of care and you are helping care for them, that is considered a pressure situation. Dick's gifting to ask questions and learn someone's story demonstrates how we can express to a person that they matter; we get to know and value them for who they are in their uniqueness.

Chip defines the human need of mattering as being valued for our uniqueness. Mattering is being cherished and cared about for the giftings, talents, and abilities that we have. It is not about the product we produce with these. It is about the person we are because of them.

How do belonging and mattering impact this topic of communicating that I care? You have probably heard some form of the saying, "Someone does not care how much you know until they know how much you care." I have heard some people add "about them" to the saying. It is the "about them" in which we are most interested because it welcomes dignity and respect into the room. People want to know we care, but not just that we care about something. When they can sense that we not only care about something, but also someone—and that someone is them— they begin to realize and know that they belong and matter.

Unfortunately, it can be challenging to keep the importance and the "why" of communicating that we care in focus, but this is paramount, as the communication of caring has a vital impact on those we are caring for. Our communication with those we care for should communicate they belong, and they matter, and they are seen and known. Anything short of this misses the mark.

Communication that demonstrates that someone belongs, matters, and is seen and known takes intentionality, a continual refocusing, and persistent effort. It takes authenticity and ingenuity because this is where the breakdown in caring can occur. We get so focused on the act of caring and forget how vitally important the communication part is.

The opposite of authentic, genuine, and intentional is canned and rote. When our communication in caring comes off as canned or rote, it communicates something to the one we are caring for. It communicates the opposite of belonging and mattering, and at times it can make the person feel like they are a burden or inconvenience. It communicates that they are only worth half your effort, a percentage of your intentionality, or maybe a "this is the best I got, take it or leave it" attitude. This is not likely anyone's desire or motive, but at the same time, what we communicate can begin to shape the other person's perception of what is going on inside of us.

That last statement may come off as harsh or brash, but I encourage you to have a transparent conversation with someone who will be honest with you. Ask them, "What am I communicating to you when I care for you?" Then ask, "Do you ever feel like I am rushed when I am caring for you, and what does that communicate to you?" Something to ask yourself is, "The last time someone cared for me, did I feel that I belonged, mattered, and was seen and known? What were some reasons I felt the way I did?"

The How and When in Communicating Care

Once we understand the why behind communicating care and the what of our communication, the next step is the how and when in communicating care.

In our world today, a plethora of ways exist to communicate that we care. They include face-to-face personal visits, phone calls, video messages, texts messages, emails, and handwritten cards. Sometimes so many options paralyze us into doing nothing. And sometimes we just get caught up thinking about the outcomes, rather than communicating so it can be received.

So, how do we choose what method of communication to use and when?

The earlier discussion about expectations and naïve realism is vitally important to what methods we use to communicate that we care. By way of illustration, I knew someone who was going through a difficult time. It was a separation that was proving to be challenging for all involved. People reached out with cards, texts, emails, personal visits, and acts of service, but when I spoke with this person, he shared that several people had not reached out at all. I was confused because I saw the cards sitting on his desk at work, including cards from the same people he said had not reached out. So, I asked him about this, and his response was, "Yes, they sent cards, but they have not visited in person." He wanted a personal visit, not just a card.

Was he being unreasonable? I don't know. But had he communicated his expectations to those around him? Probably not.

The simplest way to know what method of communication a person prefers is to ask. I am a fan of asking, and I try to ask before someone is in the middle of a challenging time. If I do not know, I will inquire from someone who knows the person well, rather than put him or her on the spot in the middle of a challenging time.

This is where the art of caring kicks in. It can seem impersonal or mechanical to ask what someone prefers in their time of need, but at first, you may just need to ask. As you grow in your ability to care, you make caring less mechanical and more of an art. If you have been paying attention, normally you know how that person communicates with you and others when they are caring for you or them. This is commonly their preferred method of communication.

I compare this to sharing with my wife that I want her to tell me she loves me every day. She would do it, I'm sure. But in the back of my mind, I would think that the only reason she is telling me this every day is because I asked her to do it. Very few people want someone to care for them out of duty. People desire for others to care for them from the heart.

I am not a mind reader. You are not a mind reader. So, if you have no other options, ask. Now, how we ask and what we offer is also very important. We will look at that more in chapter 10 when we discuss a better offer.

Choosing Which Method to Use

I like to use care pathways to help me decide how to communicate. In nursing, care pathways are proven guidelines that are applied to certain situations that help provide a more predictable outcome. The more I mentally walk through a care pathway and apply it, the more evaluative I am, and the better I become in my responses and care. When I am caring for someone else, their preferences will weigh heavier than mine. For sure, this needs to have a healthy balance. When it comes to care, the one I am caring for is at the center of this story, not me. I desire for it to remain that way.

The first question I ask myself is: How have they communicated with me in the past? Do they call me or send a WhatsApp message? Do they send me an email or handwritten card? Remember, people normally do things the way they do for a reason. So, if you can naturally bring this topic up in conversation beforehand, it helps a ton. Try a question like: "I appreciated the card you sent me. That took time and effort. Do you like to receive cards?" Maybe they hate cards and only sent it because they think that is what you like. This clears things up beforehand.

Perhaps there is not the luxury of having a conversation ahead of time, so I commonly follow their lead. If they text, I think that is what they believe is the right way to communicate. If they write cards rather than send emails, most likely they think that is the way to do it. If they call, that gives me a good clue that calling is their preferred method of communication. When in doubt, I follow their lead.

Second, I ask myself: What am I trying to communicate and how important or serious is it? If I have only ever communicated with them about surface matters, like West Virginia University football, trout fishing, or apple pie, text may be the best. But if the situation is a separation or loss of a parent, I would not choose text message. The more life-changing, altering, or impacting, the more personal I try to be. If the best I can do, due to location or time, is a video message, then I record one. If they care for others through personal visits, and I am able to visit, then this would always be my choice.

The third question I run through my mind: Is the person I am attempting to communicate care with able to receive it? At the present time, are they overwhelmed and the last thing they need is me sitting at their house? In this case, if they are overwhelmed, then a phone message might be the way to go. I can follow up with a personal visit at a later time. I never want my caring (1) to be a burden to others and (2) to be what *I* want rather than what is best for the person for whom I am trying to care. I can easily drift towards what I want and what is easiest.

Fourth, I ask myself: What are my motives for caring, and am I in the right mood to be communicating with them? People who know me know I am more like Jesus from early morning to early evening. Outside this window are not my best communication times, and I need to be aware of my emotional and mental state. If not, my act of caring can turn into "just get it over with" or "out of duty," not genuine care. If you have ever been cared for by someone who was in a hurry or doing it out of duty, you know it can cause more harm than good. Whenever I hear myself saying or thinking, "It's better than nothing," that is my warning sign. If I am using "nothing" as my measuring stick, I am not in a caring state of mind and will need to wait until I am.

Honestly, people can read through duty quickly. I have experienced what I perceived as someone caring for me out of duty and I do not want to do the same to someone else because it inflicted more hurt on me than I already felt. I do not always have the luxury of communicating in my best window of time, but I never want to do more harm or cause more pain. Checking my motives and emotional state are important.

The fifth question I ask myself is: How well do I know the person, or how well do they know me? Sometimes relationships are not congruent. For instance, a church member may feel they really know their pastor because they hear him speak most Sundays of the year. But the pastor may not know the church member as well or know all the details of their life. In such instances, where incongruences in a perceived relationship exist, I aim to be more personal rather than impersonal. I am not talking about being fake, putting on a show, or playing into unrealistic or unhealthy expectations. I am saying that if I can honor a relationship, a person, and a family in a challenging time, I do my best to do it.

Who Is Responsible for Communicating Care

In communicating that we care, the person doing the communicating is responsible for making sure communication takes place. For example, if I am caring for someone and working to communicate that I care for them, the onus is on me to do my best to communicate this message in a way that the person receiving care can understand. It might be difficult to accept that the caregiver is responsible for this; I imagine some readers out there want to push back on this already.

You might be thinking about how challenging communicating that you care can be, and you probably have a multiplicity of reasons why you believe this. We can all come up with a long list of excuses for not communicating that we care.

I have found that when I start making excuses, I am just being lazy. I make excuses to alleviate my conscience and to convince myself that I have done my best and that I am not responsible for making sure care is clearly communicated; at least that is what I find myself doing when I am trying to care for someone and not communicating it well. I shift from a caring mentality to a blame mentality, and it is just simply unkind to put more pressure or to place the blame on the one receiving care. I see it happen all the time and know it is a direction I drift myself.

Some people are just harder to care for than others are. I can label a person as angry or difficult, or as a victim, but that is the last thing a person needs in their time of need—for me to label them as angry or difficult, or as a victim. They may be all three given their circumstances, I don't know. The onus is still on the caregiver to make sure that he or she is communicating that they care. Whether the person chooses to accept the care or not is up to them.

I am not proud of my tendency to drift towards blaming others to make myself feel better about my inability to communicate that I care. In all honesty, I prefer the people that are easy to communicate with and care for. Maybe you do, too. They are easy to love and easy to reach out to and extend care. Some people are just harder to care for than others.

I am happy that some are persistent in communicating that they care because I must raise my hand as a member of the "hard to care for" crowd. I do not intentionally try to make it difficult, but as a care provider, I am very uncomfortable when on the other side of receiving care. (I am working with my counselor on this and making small steps forward, not leaps and bounds, but moving in the right trajectory.)

I'm Praying for You

I cannot tell you how many times in my life I have said this or written this. "I'm praying for you." It is so easy to say quickly in a text or an email. Many times, I have said it but not followed through with an actual prayer. So, when someone tells me they are praying, I figure they are like me. Are they actually praying? I don't know. I know they mean well but may not pray for me. They say it because it is the right thing to say at the time.

I learned a "trick" from a good friend. Rather than say, "I'll pray for you," I pray for them at that moment. Right then and there. Which means I may write a prayer in a text message and send it to them or instead of saying "prayers" or "praying for you" with the hands emoji on social media, I write the prayer out. This also may mean that I stop what I am doing and pray quietly to myself, or if I am with the person, I ask them if they would mind if I prayed for them at that moment.

> Communication that demonstrates that someone belongs and matters takes authenticity and ingenuity.

I have offered to pray for people of many different faiths in many different countries. I admit, it takes courage. It might be awkward at first, but once you get over the first few seconds, it is well worth it. It also takes great courage for them to agree to let me pray for them, which is an honor to do so. I have had very few people refuse a prayer if it is done quietly and respectfully.

My prayers are short, specific, and non-embarrassing. I am Pentecostal, but I will not embarrass the person I am praying for. That defeats the purpose. Besides, God has great hearing; He does not need me to get loud. You may feel out of your comfort zone praying for someone like this, but it does not need to be a deep theological prayer. Just a prayer from your heart letting the person know you are with them, you care, and more importantly, so does God. Once you get in the practice of praying this way, it will change you. Your sensitivity for praying for others will increase and your courage will grow.

What Happened to the Airplane

You may be wondering how the airplane story unfolded and how I found my family. I finally called another airline and was given pretty much the same issued statement: "We cannot confirm or deny the location of the airplane." I knew at the end of a call this company would ask if you were satisfied with the response you received. If you were not satisfied, it was their policy to not hang up until you were. So, I just kept saying "no." I was not satisfied and would not be satisfied until I knew where my family was.

After a few hours of this back-and-forth, the agent transferred me to a manager. The manager was kind and commented on my persistence and my unwillingness to hang up. Eventually, she told me she was not able to give details but could share that the plane had landed on Reunion Island and all souls were present and accounted for.

It was a huge relief to know they had safely landed, but I still wanted to talk with them, to put my heart and mind at ease. A pastor friend of mine in Madagascar, Luciano, contacted his pastor friend, David, in Reunion Island who went on a search for my wife and kids. When Heather and the kids entered the hotel, they spoke with the person running the front desk. He received a call at that moment and asked my wife to hold just for a minute. To his surprise and Heather's, the man on the phone was Pastor David who was calling to let them know he was there for them if needed. He also said: "Please call your husband. He is worried."

Communication is so vital to effectively and purposefully care for others. At times, communication can seem like a given or like something that is not as important as the act of caring. But we need to resist that line of thinking. The following questions will help you explore your personal communication when you are caring for others:

Starting with the Why

1. Have you ever experienced "me think" when caring for someone?

2. How can clear communication increase stability and consistency in care?

3. Who is someone you know that communicates care clearly and how can you learn from them?

The What of Communicating Care

1. How can the two of the most basic human needs of belonging and mattering guide how you communicate that you care?

2. What are some questions you can ask the person you are caring for to let them feel that they are known?

3. How can you be authentic and genuine in how you communicate that you care and avoid being canned and rote?

The How and When in Communicating Care

1. What is your preferred method of communicating that you care?

2. How could you learn beforehand about others' preferred methods of communication during a challenging time?

3. How do you know if you have effectively communicated that you care?

Choosing Which Method to Use

1. How can someone else's communication methods help you decide what method they prefer?

2. Do you communicate care differently to someone you know well versus someone you know as an acquaintance? Or do you communicate the same with everyone?

3. How can you avoid communicating that you are caring for someone out of duty rather than a genuine desire to care for them?

Who Is Responsible for Communicating Care

1. Do you agree that the one doing the care is responsible to communicate? Why or why not?

2. Have you ever made excuses on why you did not communicate well?

3. Who is someone you know that communicates care effectively? What do you like about how they communicate?

I'm Praying for You

1. Have you ever said you would pray for someone and completely forgot to do it? How can you prevent doing this in the future?

2. Could you develop a short prayer ahead of time so that when you are praying with someone, it is well thought out and meaningful?

3. Have you ever prayed for someone that was in need? How did you feel?

CHAPTER 7

Responses to Care

U pon arriving in Kenya, I looked forward to having the opportunity to care for Kenyans who had skin infections and diseases impacting their lives. Having lived and served in Africa for roughly 20 years, I knew quality skincare was not readily accessible to much of the continent's population. Certainly, there are brilliant dermatologists in Africa, but accessing them on a regular basis is cost-prohibitive for a large section of the population, so I was quite excited for the opportunity to provide dermatological care in one of the poorer areas of Nairobi, the Kibera slum.

A missionary couple, Tessa (who I happened to grow up with) and her husband Randy were kind enough to organize a dermatology clinic. Randy drove us to a church where I met one of the pastors. Randy parked his STL truck in a courtyard and we exited the gate with the pastor who guided us 30 to 50 yards down a very narrow dirt path. This path between all the houses was the only way in and out of the clinic. As we arrived, we met the nurse who ran the clinic, which was in a three-story cement block building that was still under construction. Within three minutes, someone arrived at the clinic and told us there was a fire in a house nearby. "That's an interesting start to the day," I thought.

The pastor hurried us to the second floor, telling us that fires like this happened quite frequently in Kibera. After a few minutes it was clear that the fire was growing and there was no way to escape it. No windows or doors had yet been installed on the second or third stories of the building. The space we were in was completely open to the outside with increasing amounts of smoke. At this point, I started to get nervous as the only way in and out of the clinic was down the narrow dirt path that went directly past the fire.

Suddenly, the propane tanks in the burning house exploded. I have never lived in a place at war or experienced the detonation of bombs, but the sound and feel of those propane tanks exploding was what I imagined bombs were like. I could feel the reverberations from the explosion dancing in my eardrums and through my body.

The pastor then noted that it was quite common for people to begin to loot and pillage during these fires, and he quickly became concerned for our safety not only from the fire but also from those on the street. He decided that we needed to evacuate the clinic and head towards the parked truck. We needed to go... and fast. He told us to run and not stop until we arrived at the gate where the truck was. He and another pastor insisted on taking our belongings as those on the street were less likely to attack them for the supplies.

We took off running down the narrow path, dodging the sharp, rusted edges of the tin roofs that were perilously in our way and slowing us down. To reach the truck, we had to run past the fire and through the people, but as we neared the street, we met a large crowd that pushed us closer to the fire, too close for my comfort. Though the hairs on my arm were not singed, it was close. I could feel the fire's heat on my skin.

After making our way through the crowd and arriving at the gate, we were now cornered between the burning building and its heat and smoke, the crowd gathering around us, and the gate that was too hot to touch from the fire. The gate was the only thing between us and our truck as the crowd pressed us up against it. We tried to get through the gate, but the guard would not let us in because of the crowd. We were trapped.

My heart raced as another propane tank exploded 10 yards from us. Closer to the explosion this time, the reverberations through my body were unlike anything I have ever experienced; it felt like my heart stopped beating from the shock of it all. Suddenly, an angry young man ran towards us, wielding a machete in one raised hand and demanding that we fix his other arm which was obviously broken. This was not the time or place to be fixing a broken arm. The situation was going from bad to worse.

Realizing we could not reach the truck, we started running again to get away from the crowd and the burning house. Our best chance was the Catholic church, but as we reached the church's gate, that guard would not let us in either. Our options were dwindling...and dwindling fast. Thankfully, the priest saw us and opened the gate as the crowd rapidly formed around us once again, wanting what we had in our possession. We waited at the church for an hour until it was safe to make another attempt at accessing the courtyard where the truck was parked. The angry young man with the machete and broken arm reappeared, but unlike last time, the guard let us through the gate.

I have experienced many situations in which the people I was caring for responded in a way that confused me. I have also been perplexed at the response of others towards me as I tried to care for people in their community. I envisioned people being receptive and appreciative of the care I provided and in some way wanting to protect those providing care. Sometimes their responses have been to protect the caregiver, while at other times I have had to use my running shoes to get away from the crowd.

I have pondered the different types of responses to care that I have experienced from people while trying to care for them and condensed them to four categories: fear, apathy, confidence, and trust. Let's explore each of them.

A Fearful Response

As a caregiver, you might not expect a fearful response from someone to whom you are providing care. It can sound illogical or unlikely that someone would be fearful of someone trying to care for them. You may expect just the opposite of a fearful response, perhaps a confident, thankful, and trust-filled response. However, in my experiences over the years providing care, fear is one of the most common responses I have received.

Sometimes the fearful response is overt and easy to ascertain from a person's body language or their avoidance. Other times the fearful response is covert, and when it is, the fear driving the person receiving care can be hard to pinpoint. The overt fearful responses are easier for caregivers to adapt to, but the covert ones have left me scratching my head pondering what was going on.

When we arrived in Madagascar, my wife and I were asked to take on the responsibility of an orphanage in the capital city. The non-adoptive orphanage was a partnership with the church and the mission and had been started many years earlier. The mission asked us to consider it. The orphanage needed someone to lead it, and we were young, naïve, and available.

There was a little more to it than that—it made sense on many levels. At a young age, Heather had felt called to serve in an orphanage in Africa, and I was eager to use the gifts God had given me to care for children. But Heather and I were young with two small children of our own and taking on the responsibility for 43 other children was a stretch. We prayed about it and felt peace about giving it a go. We ending up leading the orphanage until it closed 13 years later.

But even with that end in mind, know that our first visit to the orphanage did not go anything near like we thought it would.

Just before we took over responsibility of the orphanage, 23 new kids had moved in. Most had little or no interaction with people who looked like us. So, when we pulled up to the orphanage and got out of our truck, we immediately saw the fear in some of the kids' eyes. I remember one boy in particular whose eyes appeared to double in size. He started crying and took off screaming in fear and panic in the opposite direction.

We soon found out that Malagasy parents sometimes threaten their kids with the idea that white people eat Malagasy children. The threat went something like: "If you do not behave, the white people are going to come, take you, and eat you." We arrived to care for the kids, but all they saw were people coming to eat them. I could not blame them for being fearful. I would be scared too if I thought someone was coming to eat me for lunch. But over time, the kids slowly began to have confidence in our care, and the overt signs of fear dissipated.

When you encounter a fearful response to care, my encouragement is to consider that the person you are trying to care for has had past experiences with care or conceptions of care that now make them fearful of receiving care from others. Maybe someone in their past used care as a ruse to hurt them in unthinkable ways, causing more pain and hurt rather than being an agent of care and love.

I try to discern if it is possible that my role or position reminds them of the person who caused them pain or failed to care for them in a compassionate way. I also ask myself about their experience with me. Has their experience with me given them the feeling that I am not a safe person to receive care from? I also consider that the person might be fearful of receiving care from me for reasons that have nothing to do with me personally.

Whatever the reason is, it is challenging to provide care for someone who is fearful of you. As I have shared before, the center of a *caring life* is not the caregiver but the person to whom you are giving care. So, if they cannot receive care from you due to fear, finding someone who does not provoke a fearful response is paramount.

An Apathetic Response

As a caregiver, I have also experienced apathy. Apathy does not commonly have the high emotion of fear driving it. The caregiver more commonly experiences this as tampered emotions or disinterest in receiving care from the person they are caring for. I would not call the apathetic response a hopeless response; it is more like the person is not convinced that your caring will make a significant difference. It is the idea that having minimal or guarded hope is better than experiencing the hurt that comes with false hope when a situation does not change in the way envisioned.

Certainly, there are multiple reasons for an apathetic response. Reasons could include not seeing the need for you to provide care due to a lack of prior relationship or a concern that you may not understand what they are going through. People receiving care can also battle with indifference to the challenge they are experiencing; they work to protect themselves and those close to them from further disappointment.

One of the first things we noticed at the orphanage was many of the kids new to the orphanage had orangish-colored hair. This is a common sign of malnutrition, but we knew that they were now well-fed. My suspicion was that they had intestinal worms which would steal valuable nutrients from them.

I decided we needed to treat all 43 kids and the staff for intestinal worms. The treatment is easy, inexpensive, and quite effective. I explained my desire to one of the residential staff, but it was clear he was not convinced it was necessary. We chatted for a little bit, and he explained that my expectations were too high and that many kids had orange hair. He did not think it was something I needed to be very concerned about, and he was not convinced that the treatment would change anything.

Still, he agreed to give the children the medicine that evening after dinner. The next morning, I received an excited but frantic call from him. He explained that he had a half-filled bucket of worms that had made their way from different orifices of the kids' bodies. He wanted to know if I wanted to keep them or to get rid of them.

As a caregiver, sometimes the response to your care has a positive ending like this story. But I have also experienced providing care only to see the situation not change. When someone is apathetic in their response to my care, I now have a greater compassionate response than I ever have. Whatever I do, I focus on caring but not espousing false hope because

I have seen this push someone from being apathetic towards care to being fearful.

A Confident Response

I recently had a discussion on the podcast about conflict with Ron Kuest, author, leader, and conflict management specialist.[19] Ron shared many valuable thoughts and insights, but the one that jumped out the most that I have been able to apply in many areas of my life is the idea of trust and confidence. Ron said that what we commonly refer to as trust is really confidence. A confident response in a caring situation is one in which the person receiving care conveys that they believe the caregiver is reliable, accountable, dependable, and capable. The confident response does not imply that the person receiving care does not consider the motives of the caregiver or wonder if the caregiver has their best interest at heart. Those are reserved for a trustful response, which we will look at next.

When we became the leaders of the orphanage, some of the orphans were teenagers. They had questions, and rightfully so, about this young couple that was now in charge. As we got to know the teenagers, we learned that one challenge they had was the numerous bus transfers on their way to and from school in town; the number of transfers meant sometimes waiting for buses in an unsafe part of town. When they shared this with me, I responded that if they ever needed me to come and pick them up in the evening, they just had to call and I would come.

Evidently, some of the teenagers were confident that I would come if they called while others were more apathetic as they had been disappointed too many times in the past. One night, they decided to see if I was worthy of a confident response from them or if I was all talk and no action. They called me and said they needed to be picked up at a bus stop in town because there were no buses available. I got dressed and headed out to pick them up. When I showed up at the bus station, I could see the smiles of those who had placed their confidence in me. Their confidence was validated. I was reliable, accountable, dependable, and willing to live up to my word. As they got into the truck, I heard the discussion going on, and one of the leaders told me they were talking about the fact that confident ones had won that day.

Has my care always warranted a confident response? It has not. I have made countless mistakes and missteps. How the caregiver responds when they make a mistake is key.

As caregivers, when someone responds in a confident way to our care, it is a high honor and it is something to be valued. I have seen apathetic responses turn into confident responses as caregivers proved they were reliable, accountable, dependable, and capable. In addition, I have also found that to guard someone's confident response I must quickly admit when I make a mistake and seek to make amends, not by excusing my actions away but by taking responsibility and seeking a path forward.

A Trustful Response

During the interview with Ron, he also shared that genuine trust is reserved for a small subset of people. When you think about it, who in your life is reliable, accountable, dependable, and capable, *and* who you never have to consider their motives or if they have your best interest at heart? I imagine for most of us it is a limited number of people. Personally, I have only experienced trustful responses from family and close friends.

For me to expect others I am caring for to trust me completely is just not realistic or kind. At times, a confident response

If you have someone in your life who responds to you in a trustful way, cherish it.

is even a stretch for someone I have just met. Even though I know it is not realistic for someone to respond to my care in a trustful way and I know that trustful responses are limited to a small amount of people, I still feel some irritation or frustration when I am trying to care for someone and their response is less than trustful. I would think after all these years I would have changed my tendencies, but it is still a struggle for me.

Over the years serving in the orphanage, my wife and I experienced the joys and heartaches that come with seeing kids naturally progress into adulthood. We knew that living in an orphanage was not the most ideal situation for them, and there were repercussions from that. We saw great decisions and several questionable ones. Many of the kids are doing well in life and others are still trying to figure it all out. Of the 43 that grew up at the orphanage and who we had the opportunity to care for, only two responded to Heather's and my care in a consistently trustful way.

The reason I share that there were only two of the children who consistently responded to us in a trustful way is to highlight just how unique it is for someone to respond in trust. It takes both you and them to be on the same page in the relationship. The other types of responses are more one-sided. The fearful and apathetic responses are more from the one receiving care. The confident response is more about the caregiver and their character and abilities. But for a trustful response to occur, the caregiver needs to be reliable, accountable, dependable, and capable, and the one receiving care must extend an uncommon gift by not questioning the caregiver's motives or if the caregiver has their best interest at heart. I have found these types of relationships to be unique and uncommon. If you have someone in your life who responds to you in a trustful way, cherish it.

Whether it was running from the crowd in Kibera or climbing out the back window of a church in the south of Madagascar, I have learned that often the response to care will not be what you envisioned it to be. Knowing that beforehand is valuable so you can prepare for the predictable, and the predictable is that you will likely encounter a fearful, apathetic, confident, or the rare trustful response as you care for others.

DEVELOPING YOUR CARING LIFE

Being a caregiver can be challenging for many reasons, but one of the biggest challenges is managing different responses to care. With a desire to grow in a *caring life*, what role do you play in how others respond to your care? Are you willing to care for someone who responds with apathy even as you put a lot of time and effort into caring for them? When it comes to life application, I have found one of the best places to start is self-examination. Following are some questions I have for you to start that process:

A Fearful Response

1. Have you ever been fearful of someone being your caregiver?

2. If someone is fearful of receiving care, how can you respond to them?

3. How can you pray for someone who is fearful of receiving care?

An Apathetic Response

1. How do you feel when someone responds to your care in an apathetic way?

2. What does false hope mean to you, and how can a caregiver avoid giving false hope?

3. Have you ever responded to someone's care for you in an apathetic way? What were some of the reasons you responded this way?

A Confident Response

1. How do you define reliable, accountable, dependable, and capable?

2. Do you see these four traits in yourself? Would others describe you as reliable, accountable, dependable, and capable?

3. Who in your life do you respond to in a confident way?

A Trustful Response

1. Who are the people in your life that you do not question their motives or if they have your best interest at heart?

2. What can you learn from these people about a trusting response?

3. How does your definition of trust influence your actions as a caregiver?

CHAPTER 8

Caring in Leadership

Since graduating from high school, I have remained a pretty constant consumer of education. I have attended several different colleges or universities. I simply love to learn. In one of the schools I attended, I was invited to be on a student leadership team that worked directly with the administrators of the school. The students represented the school at different functions and also received leadership training along the way.

I agreed to be on the team and honestly really looked forward to the opportunity to learn and serve alongside what I perceived to be some phenomenal leaders. One of the first events to which I was invited to represent the school was a dinner hosted for alumni and donors. The dinner was pitched as an opportunity for the leaders of the school to acknowledge the current state of the school and to cast vision for its future. The student leaders were told to arrive early at the dinner so we could greet the invited guests and make sure they felt well cared for.

We arrived early, and one of the school leaders explained how we would know who to care for the most. The leader had arranged for stars to appear on the name badges. Stars fit with the evening's theme, and they appeared to be randomly scattered on the badge around the person's name. At first, it made great sense until one school leader explained how we would know who to concentrate on, who to focus our attention and care on. He explained that anyone with five or more stars on their badge had major money, and whatever the person needed or wanted, it was our job to serve them and meet their requests. Anyone with three or four stars had a moderate amount of money, and we should do our best to care and help them if the needs of the five-star attendees were already met. He then explained that some people had one or two stars with a moon or other decoration on their badge. He said these people had little money to give and we really did not need to concentrate on them or try to care for them beyond what was already provided.

I am the son of a railroader. I was born and raised in a middle-class family that had what we needed but not extra. My parents sacrificed and gave to others above and beyond their means. I knew if I or a family member attended that dinner, we would have the one- or two-star badge and would have been in the "you do not really need to care for them" category.

The leadership lesson I learned that day from the actions of the leader was that misguided leaders care for people based on what those people have to offer them. I was not young or naïve at the time. I understood that schools run like businesses and need money. If you run a business or lead a church, I understand money is a necessity to make the business run or to fulfill a mission. I get that. But when we pseudo-care for people, making them objects to overcome or manipulate for our gain, we are in trouble. In that moment I resolved in my heart that when I became a leader, I would remember the lesson I learned that day and not fall into the trap of pseudo-care.

For leaders to care for those they serve, they must establish confidence and trust with them. Executive leadership coach Mike Messner notes that the way we build confidence and trust is through trustworthy behavior, through actions that demonstrate that we are reliable and accountable leaders of integrity.[20] The pseudo-care that I observed at that dinner that night did not build confidence and trust, but rather created apathy towards the school and a level of fear towards the leader. After what I experienced, I would have never had enough confidence in that leader to allow him to care for me.

Parents, coaches, CEOs, and managers, many eyes are watching as you care for others. They are watching and observing more than you think they are. It has been said that the true test of character is how you treat those who can offer you nothing in return. A better judge of character is the difference between how we care for those who can do much for us in return and those who can offer nothing in return. We can fool ourselves saying that we treat everyone the same. I have not seen that to be true. Try this. Give yourself a score from 1 to 10 (10 being the best quality of care) on how you care for those who can help you immensely. Next, score yourself on how you care for those who have nothing to offer you. The distance between those two numbers reveals something, and seeing the difference between the two is a more accurate measure of our caring character. I would submit that the greater the difference between the numbers, the weaker one's character is.

Are you a leader that only cares for those that help you meet your goals and deadlines, or help you realize your vision? Or are you a leader that strives to care for people and treat them with dignity no matter how many stars they have on their name tag?

Leaders have a phenomenal opportunity to demonstrate the importance of care by normalizing and modeling how they are cared for, the language they use in their care for others, and the actions they take in caring for those around them. With leadership comes great responsibility—and it creates great dysfunction if we separate the two. As a leader, how are you modeling care, how does your language demonstrate care, and are your actions above reproach on how you care and treat others?

Caring and Vulnerability

It was a balmy September day in Madagascar. I was driving to the local clinic where I served and practiced dermatology. I love to maximize my time, so more often than not, I listen to podcasts while I drive.

This particular day was no different, and the podcast I was listening to was an interview with Erwin McManus. I briefly met Erwin in Senegal a few years earlier when he came to teach leadership to the workers I serve with in Africa. He is a creative, visionary thought leader, master communicator, creative genius, and author, among other things. Through his books and his teachings, I have learned that he has quite a unique, God-given talent to see a situation from multiple perspectives, to process each perspective, and then to eloquently communicate those perspectives.

On the podcast, he shared a concept that I had experienced but never had the words to describe, and he described it so eloquently. He shared that leaders are often very invested in those they serve because they believe in them and desire to see them grow. In the process, a leader can give to, care for, buy meals for, and pray for the one he serves. He gives a part of his life to this person. Through this, the leader can develop a profound and real sense of loyalty to a person and, at times, that person's family. The challenge then arises when the person being served does not give to, care for, buy meals for, or pray for the leader, and in the process, does not develop the loyalty to the leader that the leader has towards the one being served. *Wow!* That describes the experiences that business leaders, pastors, and parents have had for a long time. An unequally yoked loyalty. When the person walks away from the leader or has an opportunity to care for the leader and does not, hurt and bewilderment result.

Humans in general try to avoid hurt and confusion. Leaders can do this even more so as they move away from vulnerability towards a perceived sense of control. In essence, leaders can build walls to protect themselves from others.

In my life experience, some of the people that I have cared for the most have been the ones that have hurt me the deepest—whether they withdrew from the relationship, criticized the way I cared for them, or just "ghosted" me, moving on with little to no explanation. Each and every time, it hurt. It hurts because I gave a part of my life to care for them and thought some sense of loyalty had developed between us.

If you are a leader that has cared for those you serve and you have been hurt, you are not alone. It is uncomfortable for me to be with those I serve as they care for or buy me a meal, but following Erwin's advice from that day's podcast, I have had to get over it. As a leader, I needed to grow in my emotional maturity, as my coach says. If I do not get over it, and I do not allow them to care for me, I foster a one-way loyalty in my caring and build walls to avoid future hurt and not care for others.

Leader, my question for you is: How do you let other people care for you? And if you do not, what are some of the reasons that you do not? Have you been hurt? Are you like me and do not like to admit the vulnerability that you need to be cared for?

Leaders are courageous. That is just who leaders are. They are people with the courage to serve others, knowing they may be hurt in the process. One of the greatest acts of courage you will demonstrate to the team you serve, the family you love, or the employees you lead is when you dare to let others care for you. That is the case for me. My most courageous moments are not when I act independently, but rather when I admit I need help and receive care from others.

> One of the greatest acts of courage you will demonstrate is when you dare to let others care for you.

Corporate culture's idea and description of a leader is most likely different. Who I am as a leader would probably be considered weak. But I am convinced that as a leader it takes a lot more courage to receive care than to give it. To be clear, I am not talking about being a self-absorbed leader who makes everything about them and is in constant need.

Leaders model. Leader, what you model is what you will reproduce. If you model being cared for and responding to that care with thankfulness, loyalty, and appreciation, you will be able to transfer that DNA to those you serve. If you choose not to, that is your choice, and you will replicate that choice also.

Reframing Organizational Management Lingo

Our friends, the Maddox family, used to live in Jerusalem. While they were there, we had the opportunity to spend some unforgettably rich times with them, including tours of the most common biblical sites.

Interestingly enough, one memory that sticks out in my mind the most is visiting Hezekiah's tunnel. Built by King Hezekiah in 701 B.C., this 1,750-foot tunnel was cut in the bedrock of the City of David to bring water from one side of the city to the other. For a guy like myself who could not dig a small trench on top of the ground and expect to meet someone in the middle, I found this engineering marvel truly amazing.

As my family walked through this deep underground tunnel with our friends, I wondered if this was the smartest thing we had ever done. Our kids were small, and the water came up to at least their knees and at times higher. For anyone who is claustrophobic, this is not the walk for them—this space was *narrow*. One thing I did not expect (not that I put much consideration into this whole thing before doing it, truth be told) was the sound in the tunnel. My voice and everyone else's voices reverberated through the tunnel. It was hard to hear. Even hearing what the person in front of me said was hard. The voices and sounds of the people in the tunnel reverberated all around.

As a leader, the language and word choices you choose create stronger reverberations than you may imagine. Our language ripples through the hearts and minds of those we serve far longer than the few seconds it takes to utter them. The language we use as leaders as we model caring for others resounds.

I cringe a little inside when I hear leaders and organizations talk about the processes, structures, and systems they have in place to care for the families, teams, and employees they serve. I understand the use of these terms in operations management, but not in the care for people. I am not proposing we get rid of these words, but I do suggest not using them when it comes to caring for human beings. When I think of systems, I think of the production of bottles and cars and computers. I think of the juvenile detention system, the prison system, the educational system, the social security system, etc. The words system, structure, and process do not make me think of caring and human dignity.

The use of the system, structure, and process language communicates uniformity and standardization, which works well for inanimate objects with no humanity or soul, with no emotions, feelings, responsibilities, or inherent dignity. The intent of the language is going in the right direction because it shows a desire for consistency and stability. But when we care for people, they can hear. They listen consciously and unconsciously to what we say and the language or verbiage we choose to communicate it.

In the turbulent, unsettling days in which we live, consistency and stability in leaders are two things those we serve are looking for. Consistency allows someone to know how they will be cared for and decreases stress and anxiety. When leaders provide stability, it creates the environment for those they serve to grow in trust of the organization and its leaders.

Leaders desire to communicate consistency, but the use of system, structure, and process language communicates uniformity, not consistency, and uniformity and consistency do not have the same meanings. Uniformity conveys the idea that everything is the same and identical, and diversity in care is not a desired outcome. A system with diversity is seen as an error, an anomaly. Uniformity lacks the acknowledgment of individual circumstances and personal situation.

When we care for people, it is extremely difficult to communicate understanding and care when there is no consideration for the realities of being human or of individual circumstances. Think of a time you registered for something, and the business was more interested in your number in their system than they were in your name. How did it make you feel? My guess is you felt less than human and uncared for.

> **The language we use as leaders as we model caring for others resounds.**

In my journeys, I have never met a person who wants their care to be systemized, or at least they do not want it communicated that way. Those we serve want leaders who have forethought and a game plan. When leaders envision, design, and implement care for those they serve, they must carefully consider their use of terms and how those terms communicate care.

When we use system and structure language, we send a message to those we serve that they are a commodity to be managed, not a human to be valued and served. I know that is not the message leaders want to send. Most leaders are not nefarious, looking to eliminate human dignity, but if we are not careful with our language, the very thing we are aiming to do—care for those we serve—becomes distorted.

One last thing on our language, leaders, I caution you to consider how you talk about the team members, colleagues, or employees you serve. The system, structure, and process mindset can bleed over into how we talk about and ultimately care for others. My dad worked at the railroad as an electrician for 43 years. He could come home and talk about engines, electrical components, crossties, and railroad tracks all he wanted without any of those things being hurt by the language he used. My grandfather was a farmer and raised chickens for their eggs. He could talk all he wanted about eggs, chickens, and feed. On the other hand, my mom was a nurse, and she did *not* talk about those she cared for. She knew that the children and families she had the honor of caring for had emotions, stories, feelings, and dignity.

Leaders, sometimes we think we can talk about the people we serve as my dad did about the railroad engines, crossties, and electrical components. It is impossible to communicate care if we talk about the people we serve as if they were tools for our end game. Certainly, we can talk about people in this way but just because we can do something does not make it the respectable thing to do. If the person I serve is being challenged by the culture of our team, talking about him or her to others I serve with rather than talking to them directly conveys he or she is no more valuable than my dad's crossties and my grandfather's chickens. When we talk about those we serve in this way, it depersonalizes them. Even if it makes you feel better in the moment, you are slowly eroding trust, both internally with the team you serve on and externally with the team members, church members, or employees who observe you.

My, Mine, and Ours

Maybe you picked up on how I am learning to not use possessive pronouns when I talk about people. I do not always get it right, but I am trying to change my language. I have had the opportunity, thanks to my friend Dick Foth, to interview great leaders: Navy Admiral Vern Clark on covenant leadership and how he focused on retention and attrition in the Navy, and former United States Attorney General John Ashcroft on leading and caring for others in turbulent times. I took many golden nuggets from my time learning from them, but one of the most valuable was the importance they both placed on the language they used to describe those they served with. In contrast, I have met other leaders who call themselves servant leaders, but their descriptive language contradicts the servant part of their leadership. When leaders use possessive pronouns to describe those they serve in their home, work, or in the field, does that convey servant leadership?

It is the human condition to place ourselves in the center of every story and situation. It is the natural drift. This comes out when we use possessive pronouns as we talk about those we serve and care for: my personal assistant, my employees, my team, my fill-in-the-blank. We possess cars, houses, clothes, and other things for a certain amount of time, but we never possess people. I do not think all leaders are conveying that the people they serve with are possessions, but at times that is what the people being led and cared for hear them say. Maybe in your culture there might not be an issue in using a possessive pronoun to describe someone, but how does the other person's cultural experience perceive it?

You are probably thinking, "That is not what I mean when I say that. You are taking my words out of context or interpreting them inaccurately. I prefer to use the active voice and get directly to the point." And I accept your pushback. I am actually happy you are pushing back. It means I got you thinking.

But I firmly believe that when we use possessive pronouns to talk about people, our choice of language is communicating something to ourselves, consciously and unconsciously, and to others. The message our choice of language communicates might be different than we think and might have unintended consequences for both you and them. When a leader uses possessive pronouns to describe those they serve, are they unintentionally creating unconscious, unspoken, not-agreed-upon, or unrealistic expectations? And if a leader is creating expectations and assumptions, the responsibility to clarify what these are is the responsibility of the leader, not those the leader serves.

I challenge you to listen the next time you are in a room with people you work or serve with and see the reactions of others when a leader or manager uses possessive pronouns to describe those they serve. Take notice of how different cultural backgrounds interpret the use of possessive pronouns. And the next time you have the opportunity to watch the faces of those you serve when you make some small changes like this, you may be surprised.

As the leader, you might be trying to communicate that the person belongs and matters and that you are a highly responsible and loyal leader. You may feel like you are conveying to those you serve that they are part of a greater vision and brighter future, and that they are truly cared for by you, the leader. But some may still have feelings of being a cog in the wheel, of being a commodity, of being managed and controlled for the purpose of accomplishing the leader's vision.

Take an inventory of your own emotions the next time your coach calls you "her player" or your boss calls you "her worker."

$\vee$

A small shift in wording portrays a vastly different message.

What emotions do you feel? Are you angry, glad, sad, or hurt? I imagine your feelings and response will be different if your coach says about you: "She is the player I have the opportunity to coach" rather than "she is my player." A change in our language communicates that someone holds great value and is not something to possess. A covenant or servant leader is not at the center of the story, and he or she does their best to communicate that.

Language is important: the office assistant I serve with, the team members I serve and work with, the employees I serve with and care for. It is a small shift in wording, but a small shift in wording portrays a vastly different message than using possessive pronouns to describe those we care for. The shift in wording takes the leader from the center of importance and puts the person they serve in the place of importance.

Now, what about family? With our children and our spouses, the use of possessive pronouns can communicate a sense of belonging and responsibility which are vital, and I am all for communicating that we have a place where we matter and belong. But as any parent whose child has moved out or any spouse who has gone through a divorce knows, we can steward a relationship, but we are never truly owners of the people. We do not control others, even those in our family.

So, what does the use of possessive pronouns communicate deep down to those in our family? This is a great question for those you love and serve in the family environment. It is not for me to decide how they feel or perceive the use of your language, but I think it is a great question to ask spouses, children, or extended family: What do you think and feel when I say you are my husband or my wife or my son or my daughter?

As leaders, making changes in the language we use in how we communicate our care for others will bring major changes in morale, team cohesion, and the bottom line (whatever your bottom line is). When we remove the possessive pronoun and put the person first, we will be speaking their heart language. When the emphasis is on them and not on us, they will know that they belong and they matter, and we are with them.

Importance of Follow-Up

Leaders know that in whatever arena one leads, follow-up is paramount. We know the importance of following up with business contacts or clients, and it is common practice for pastors to follow up with those who visit a church. Coaches follow up with those being recruited for the team, and parents know the value of having follow-up conversations with children.

But when it comes to caring, we can forget about the importance of follow-up. When something just happens—divorce, loss of a loved one, job furlough, or new diagnosis—there is a rush of support and care. Over time, the expression of care and concern diminishes because we do not know what else to say or do, our lives move on, and/or another challenge arises somewhere else. Another reality is that leaders do not stop leading; whatever they are engaged in, those responsibilities do not stop.

My challenge for leaders is when it comes to follow-up, use the same intentionality employed in other arenas. Apply intentionality to your follow-up in caring for those you serve. An old risk management slogan says, "If it's predictable, it's preventable." The hurt that comes with the lack of follow-up is predictable, and if leaders are intentional about follow-up, the hurt is largely preventable. I have seen people go through a tragedy only to feel forgotten, unseen, unheard, and undervalued because follow-up was lacking or at times non-existent.

Leaders, the message we send when we fail to follow up with those we serve is not only sent to that person or family. The others you serve are also paying attention; they observe and note your response. Their observation may be out of concern for their colleague or friend, but as I noted earlier, we normally see ourselves at the center of the story, so they will connect the dots and make a mental note of what to expect from their leader when they face a challenge.

In my experience, it is human nature to go to the lowest, not the highest, opinion when one is making observations and linking those observations to a vision of how they will be cared for. Sometimes observations are correct, while at other times they merely amount to conspiracy theories and confabulations. Author and speaker Dr. Brene Brown talks about the danger of conspiracy theories, which have few factual data points. The danger is that people fill in the gaps of a story with their opinions and values whether true or not. Leaders, we can help curb conspiracies by filling in gaps with truth rather than leaving space for each person to speculate.

One opportunity we have to circle back and fill the gaps is with follow-up. Follow-up takes time. It takes intentionality and planning. Follow-up is an often overlooked and neglected opportunity, and when neglected it will produce weeds no one wants in the organization they lead. If we do not fill in gaps with the truth, we leave room for those we serve to fill those gaps with opinions that can lead to feelings of being unseen, unheard, and undervalued. These opinions and perspectivescan be highly contagious and will spread through an organiza- tion with great rapidity. And we wonder why loyalty to organizations and missions is at an all-time low.

People Whisperer

I noted a common occurrence in my travels to the rural areas of Madagascar. No matter the size of the village, there was commonly a village drunk or a demon-possessed person. If we were really lucky, we got both. At times, one or the other entered the mobile clinic or stood in front of the crowd while my friend Jay shared the good news of Jesus. At best, they merely distracted those who waited or participated. At other times, they could be a threat or intimidation for those who came to serve. The villagers often just laughed nervously, but for outsiders it was unsettling.

A young man often traveled with us who I noticed had a unique gifting and talent. We called him the "people whisperer." When the village drunk got unruly or started intimidating those serving, Rado often walked up, spoke kindly to him, put his arm around him, and slowly moved him away from the crowd. I did not have the courage to do this, nor was my Malagasy intelligible enough, but Rado had the gift of seeing and understanding people from a vantage point I just did not have.

Leader, you need to find a Rado, a people whisperer. Leaders can be distant from those they serve for a multiplicity of reasons including financial, positional, or geographical. I don't think the reason really matters, but what I do know is you need someone you have confidence in that sees and understands the human perspective and thinking. You need someone you trust to help you process and share what they observe, hear, and sense in the lives of those you are responsible to serve. Ultimately, it will help you better care for those you serve and will also make you a better leader.

Inspiring Those We Serve to Care

I enjoy reading books, specifically history books. One book I read recently was on Winston Churchill and the impact he had on the minds and hearts of those he served during World War II.[21] A journalist interviewed him and asked about how he gave the people of London the courage to endure the war and to come out victorious.

Churchill quickly corrected the journalist and shared that he had not given the people courage; rather, he had focused the courage they already had. He was able to help them focus the courage that was in them to overcome the fear and push towards victory.

As leaders desiring to care for those we serve, Churchill's words should ring true to us also. Leaders have the opportunity to inspire and create an environment that helps focus the courage of those we serve so they can care for those around them. We get what we celebrate. If we celebrate the courage in each of us when we care for others, we can truly impact the communities we live and serve in.

Leaders, be courageous yourself and beware of the trap of "how I model care for those I serve is better than nothing." Measuring our actions and how we care against nothing is a pretty low standard and is not courageous. That is like saying: My model of care is better than hurting others and doing absolutely nothing. Is that really our aim? Focus on your courage and measure your care against a high standard, not nothing.

DEVELOPING YOUR CARING LIFE

You have probably heard it said that everything rises and falls on leadership. Caring is no different. As a leader, how you care for those you serve will be replicated in those you lead. The following questions will be a great start as you navigate this tremendous responsibility that goes with leadership:

Caring and Vulnerability

1. How does the phrase "unequally yoked loyalty" sit with you? Have you experienced this?

2. What are some ways that leaders can resist isolating themselves when someone they have cared for hurts them?

3. What leader comes to mind when you think of a leader who cares and is vulnerable?

4. When a leader receives care, what does that demonstrate to those around them?

Reframing Organizational Management Lingo

1. As a leader, what does your language or verbiage communicate to those you serve? What are some ways you could change your language to communicate that you genuinely care?

2. Within the organization you lead, have you clearly thought out the difference between uniformity and consistency? Do your strategies to care for those you serve communicate uniformity or consistency?

3. What other words can you utilize to communicate that you care other than words like systems and processes?

4. When you talk about those you serve, what are you communicating—respect, love, and appreciation?

My, Mine, and Ours

1. In what ways do you use possessive pronouns concerning those you serve?

2. What do you communicate when you use possessive pronouns?

3. Do you believe it is important to limit the use of these possessive pronouns to communicate value and care to those you serve?

Importance of Follow-Up

1. Do you have a plan in place to follow up with those you serve after they have been through a challenging time?

2. When it comes to follow-up, how important is it to you personally? Are you using that personal conviction to impact the DNA of the organization?

3. Have you had someone follow up with you after you have been through a challenging time? Is that motivation enough for you to follow up with others?

People Whisperer

1. Do you know someone with an innate ability to communicate with others and to connect with people?

2. If you do not have a "people whisperer" speaking into your leadership decisions, what are some reasons you are resistant to this?

3. What would you need to have in place to help you trust someone so that you can better understand those you serve?

Inspiring Those We Serve to Care

1. Does your leadership inspire others to be courageous in how they care for others?

2. Where do you find your courage to care for others—internally, externally, or both?

3. Who do you know that is courageous in how they care, and for what reasons?

CHAPTER 9

Source of Caring

On yet another trip to a rural area of Madagascar, we encountered the military, and they were not so happy with us. We had flown down to the southeast coast of the island to do a medical clinic with the aim of encouraging pastors and the local community. This time we traveled to the village with Helimission, a missions agency that uses helicopters to reach hard-to-access locations. Everything had gone pretty well until we were ready to leave the "airport." I say "airport" because it was unlike a Western airport. A closer description would be a parking lot with a railroad track running through it and cows grazing in the grass. This was our runway.

We loaded up in the helicopter. I was exhausted, and as the pilot began his checks, I saw in the corner of my eye a pickup truck full of military guys waving weapons. They were pointing at us and appeared to be shouting. Helicopters are loud, so the shouting part is a guess. We all acknowledged them, but we were still not convinced they had come for us. I thought maybe they had come to say goodbye and thank us for helping the community. I was wrong on that count.

The pilot slowly put the helicopter back down and got out to show the military guys that he had followed all the rules and had all the necessary documentation. They were not so convinced, and it became evident that the situation was escalating quickly. They were carrying AK-47s, which they then pointed and waved at the pilot. As usual, we had no weapons. The pilot had military training, so he was not intimidated one bit, while I was still in the helicopter and thoroughly intimidated. I admit it: I am not accustomed to guys waving AK-47s at me.

As it became more and more evident that this situation would not be resolved any time soon, the doctor I served with got out of the helicopter to see if he could mediate a solution. He approached a few of the military guys who immediately surrounded him. They all appeared to have attended the School of Fear and Intimidation as they used the same tactics on the doctor as they had on the pilot—pointing guns, screaming, hollering, and making all kinds of accusations.

As I watched this unfold, I had a few options as I saw it. Stay in the safety of the helicopter, call for help, or get out and see if I could make sense of what was going on. For some odd reason, I thought I could help calm the situation down, so I got out of the helicopter and approached one of the soldiers. I did not pick well; I picked the mean drunk one.

His nose was close enough to my face that I could have licked it. This was before COVID-19 and masks, but I am not stupid. I am not in the habit of licking noses, let alone the nose of a mean military guy. He asked me why I had come to the village and what my reason was for being there. I knew that when someone is yelling at me, it rarely helps to yell back. Besides, he had a big gun.

I calmly explained that we came to work and provide free medical care. I did not mention the pastor or his name because I did not want him drawn into the situation if possible. The military man was not satisfied with my answer. He had a suspicion that I was some hired gun or mercenary. I do not know, maybe it was the sunglasses or the short hair. I tried to explain that I was in no way a mercenary, and if I was one, I would be horrible at it.

He was not amused. He responded that foreigners like me thought they could come and do whatever they wanted, pretend like they were caring for patients, give away a little medication, and then take advantage of the people. Which in his defense, he was not wrong; people do take advantage of these situations.

But he was clearly in a bad mood, and reasoning with someone who is unreasonable has rarely ever done much good. I was in his path, and there was not a clear way out of it other than to stand and listen to him.

I have many such stories of people questioning my motives when trying to care for people. I wish I could say that I can always let these moments roll off my back, that I could compartmentalize and forget about it, pretending that it does not bother me and it is no big deal. But in reality, these circumstances are like a slow leak that cause more irritation with each drip.

Unless I can replace what I give out, I eventually run dry.

The Fool's Choice

Growing up I often heard people say, "I would rather burn out than rust out." For a long time, I agreed with this statement. Burnout reflected the Appalachian culture in which I grew up. A culture that valued action and movement. A life in motion was the sign of a productive life. The mindset of "doing something even if it is wrong," as my dad commonly said, was a phrase that often ran through my mind. If I had to choose, I did not want to rust out.

Where I grew up, one of the most insulting things to say to someone was to call them lazy. Rusting out due to lack of action, movement, and advancement was a cardinal sin, something to be avoided at all costs. Interestingly enough, people's love language reflected acts of service because action and work were valued. If someone was caring for you, they were doing something for you, not just saying or thinking something. For a while, I was convinced that burning out was the best option.

But was that my only choice?

As I heard people say, "I would rather burn out than rust out," I understood this to mean there were only two choices: Choice #1 was sitting still, self-preserving, doing nothing, and being viewed as lazy, and choice #2 was running so hard that I had nothing left to give, broken-down physically, emotionally, and spiritually. At first, burnout sounded courageous. It carried some sense of a sacrificial warrior or suffering servant. But many of those I knew who had burned out were mere shells of the people they were prior to the burnout. And it was a long journey back for those who were able to recover from their burnout. The physical, emotional, and spiritual costs and consequences of burnout almost made me think being called lazy might be the better choice.

Maybe it was the better choice.

But as I have grown older and watched people burn out as they care fast and furious for others, while some sit on the sidelines consumed with self-preservation for fear of how caring for others will impact them, I began to search for other options.

There had to be better options. Burning out or rusting out seemed like a fool's choice.[22]

⌄

Choosing between burning out or rusting out is a fool's choice.

A fool's choice is when we put ourselves in a box or paint ourselves into a corner and we feel, perceive, and believe that we only have two real options. We feel pressured, whether internally or externally, to choose between two options, an "either this or that" decision. Even if neither option is a good option, we feel we must choose one of them. Choosing between burning out or rusting out is a fool's choice.

I have not met anyone on my life's journey who likes to be called a fool. Me included. No one likes their decisions to be considered foolish. But that is exactly where we end up if we make caring for others an either-this-or-that, burn-out-or-rust-out fool's choice. We make a foolish decision.

Because there are better options.

I had the pleasure of walking through Al Toledo's *DNA of a Leader* [23] with the leaders I serve with in the Indian Ocean basin. Al shared a quote from Chuck Swindoll that truly resonated with me: "If you burn out or rust out, you are still OUT."

I don't know about you, but my life goal has never been to be out. I never wanted to strike out or be thrown out in baseball. I never wanted to foul out in basketball. I never wanted to be ruled out of bounds in football, cross country, or track. I never wanted to sit in time-out as a kid. I never wanted to not be chosen or left out when interviewing for a job. And I have never wanted to be out professionally, washed out to the point that I could barely care for myself, let alone other people, depleted of my joy and love for others.

Even though I have avoided "being out" both personally and professionally, in recent years it appears the desire to "be out" has become more tempting and appealing than it has ever been. We only have to look at the professions of caring and service like nurses, pastors, social workers, missionaries, doctors, teachers, police officers, and counselors. The desire to "be out" is glaringly evident when you consider the rising rates of depression, anxiety, and suicide. It is a desire to do something or be somewhere else. Do not get me wrong. Caring professions have always had a high rate of burnout and turnover; it comes with the territory. But in the last few years, "being out" has been up and to the right.

Although this book is not specifically focused on caring professionals, we can definitely learn from them and the recent trends. The last few years have seen increased rates of caring professionals walking away from the professions they loved, felt called to, and sacrificed time, energy, and finances to be a part of. They are walking away because they are frustrated and depleted. With the compounding effects of COVID-19, politics, and face-to-face encounters with the injustices in our culture, caring professionals have burned out. We may not use those words, but that is what has happened and is happening.

Burnout should not necessarily assign negative motives, lack of self-discipline, or character flaws to a person. Honestly, it is probably the inverse. Someone cares with the best of intentions, and slowly the leak happens. The reality is the slow leak can and most likely will happen if we care for others. If we are not intentional about replacing by replenishing, we burn out. Reaching burnout is the reality that one can only give what one has. If what one has is not restored, replenished, reenergized, and refreshed, one will eventually deplete to empty, bankrupt emotionally, physically, and spiritually with nothing left to give.

What can we do to not "be out"? Knowing the challenge and the reality that caring depletes, what can we do? When we are replenished, recharged, reenergized, and refreshed, it is more difficult to burn out or rust out. Unless we continually refill, we will eventually run out.

And what can those who desire to care for others do? How can they avoid making a fool's decision between burning out and rusting out? How can someone avoid both depletion and self-preservation? All great questions and the subject of many books, podcasts, webinars, and lectures. The information on burnout is there. That is not the problem or challenge.

The first challenge I run into is accepting that the information and research apply to me, that I am *not* somehow exempt, unique, or special. I wish I was, but I am not.

The second challenge is that once I accept that I am not unique or exempt, I must put the knowledge I gain into action. How do I change my habits? How do I change what I value? How do I practically recognize that I have limits? The foundational conclusion I have come to in the immortal words of the priest in the movie *Rudy*, "There is a God, and I am not Him."

Caring Requires a Source

The idea of having a source to fill us up as we care for others is common and accepted. There are not many people who will argue with the concept that you cannot give what you do not have (except perhaps some politicians and the federal government). It is impossible to possess someone else's mental, emotional, spiritual, and physical energy and strength. It is theirs, not mine. I cannot borrow from someone's storage of strength. It is not transferable.

Still, even with the acknowledgment that we need a source and that we cannot give what we do not have, how do we find the source? It is less common today for people to pursue a healthy lifestyle of replenishment. We have a theoretical understanding of the importance of replenishment, but we fail to do anything about it practically.

The focus of this book is a *caring life*, and you and I cannot care well for someone if we have nothing with which to care. This is not about the financial resources of caring. This is more about the emotional, spiritual, and physical energy and capacity to care for someone.

One of the first books I read on this subject was Wayne Corderio's book *Leading on Empty*. I was a younger man at the time with more energy than common sense. We were living in Madagascar, and I was staying up all night for class working on my doctorate in nursing and trying to live my days as if I was sleeping at night. I was not sleeping, which made the charade hard to pull off.

My wife and I had two small kids at home. We oversaw an orphanage, and I frequently traveled to the bush to care for people's physical and spiritual needs. I continually added on, but never removed anything at all. When I had momentum, people recognized the momentum and wanted to jump on. They wanted to share all of their good ideas on what more I could do, on how I could make their dreams a reality, and on how I should spend the little free time I had left.

Wayne's book was the right book at the right moment in my life. It challenged me to do an intentional self-analysis of where my source was and to question whether I honestly believed my pace in caring for others was sustainable.

Since then, I have read great books and listened to countless podcasts that discuss burnout and how to avoid it. But is that the best we can do when it comes to caring for others? Just avoid burnout? Numerous authors, speakers, and leaders have well-thought-out hypotheses on burnout. Their ideas range from the extreme to the simple. Some say to do only what self-actualizes, energizes, recharges, and refreshes you (which is out of reach for the majority of the world). Others advise you to sacrifice throughout daily life, but with periods of the day that focus on the need to reenergize, recharge, and refresh (which can also seem hard to reach and make life sound like drudgery).

Some recommend stepping away or removing oneself from the caring situation, even suggesting extended sabbaticals and long vacations as ways to recharge and refill after spending extended time caring for others.

Some suggest that consistent exercise, better sleep, and better nutrition and hydration are the keys to replenishing our bodies, souls, and minds. The basic principles of exercise, diet, hydration, and sleep are very valuable. But there is personal variation in what is restorative in sleep, exercise, diet, and hydration—and we like to exploit the variation. At least I do. In fact, I have seen those who are bent towards burnout (myself included) make excuses that they are unique—true anomalies and wondrous machines designed by God who only need minimal sleep, can eat apple pie as a food group, hydrate with corn syrup and caffeine-laced drinks only, and exercise by moving forks to their mouths. These unicorns can care for others no matter the circumstances because the practices of replenishing simply do not apply to them. Unfortunately, I have seen how these stories end. Unicorns are not real.

I like what author and podcaster Carey Nieuwhof shares that "time off will not heal you when the problem is how you spend time on."[24] If I am caring for others in unhealthy ways and if I depend on myself rather than a true source in my "time on," eventually I will be in trouble. If I am not replenished while caring for others, I will eventually run dry. It is not sustainable.

As we care for others, we pour out, which I believe is what each of us is called to do. If you are a Jesus follower, I am certain that is what you are called to do. The apostle Peter wrote that we should each use whatever gift we have to serve others (1 Peter 4:10), and in the Gospels, we see Jesus compassionately caring for others over and over. To pour one's life out is synonymous with being a Christian, regardless of what popular Christianity might lead us to believe. We, in our own strength, cannot fill up in a week what took us months to pour out. We need to follow the example of Jesus and continually refill our tanks.

It is not the pouring out that is in question. Pouring out in caring for someone has to happen. What is in question is how we replenish what we poured out. We see Jesus being continually replenished by His Father, but as we care for others, we drift from daily replenishing ourselves. We think a week's vacation or a few days off will fill us up. So, what about those who cannot take expensive vacations? What about those caring for a loved one without the financial means to go away for a time of rest and replenishment?

One-Minute Vacations

Many of you reading this book know exactly what I mean when I say that some people do not have the finances, time, or job flexibility to take extended vacations for replenishment. Among us are the bi-vocational pastor of a small church, working an evening job to make ends meet because the church cannot pay him enough to raise a young, growing family; and the plumber who works six days a week most weeks to help his college-age kids through school; and the single parent with one income who simply does not have the time and space in this season of her life.

We can admit to scrolling through Instagram and Facebook and seeing another pastor, a former school friend, or a two-parent, two-income family, and fighting the jealousy of their extravagant vacations and times of rest. They may have good intentions in their post to promote a healthy lifestyle, but their photos just make us realize how far we are from making that a reality in our lives. We all would love to take the same vacations to recharge, reenergize, and replenish, but it is just not possible and way out of reach.

If your goal is to truly replenish, my friend and mentor Mark Lehmann has a solution that has been truly valuable for him. He takes one-minute vacations. One-minute vacations are stepping away mentally and physically to a restful place. We can take one-minute vacations multiple times a day, and one of the best parts is…they're free! They may not make the Instagram or Facebook feed, but they can truly be a way to replenish during the day. So, maybe your way to refresh, recharge, and replenish will be a one-minute vacation. Perhaps that is what you can afford and make work in this season of life. In these one-minute segments, you can be replenished. It works for Mark and could work for you.

I like to run. Though as I have gotten older, it falls more into the jogging category, and the walking category is probably not far off. My morning runs are normally four or five miles long, but in my younger days, I ran some longer distances and races. I learned a lot about myself, my body, and my mental capacity on those long training runs.

One lesson I learned as I prepared for the Disney marathon was that I could run between seven and eight miles without drinking or eating anything. My body could maintain a pretty good pace with the food and water I ate the night before or the morning of. If I ran longer than this without eating, I began to feel lightheaded, dizzy, grouchy, and irritable, and my pace dramatically slowed down. My gait also got off and I found I was more prone to tripping, stumbling, falling, and getting hurt.

I am not always the quickest learner, so after a pretty nasty fall and the embarrassment that followed, I took inventory of what was going on. I recognized that if I drank small amounts and ate small amounts of carbs and protein, say at miles 4, 8, and 12, then I could maintain pace and not feel dizzy, lightheaded, or grouchy. To run farther and maintain pace, water and food were vital.

The reason I did not like to drink and eat during long runs was that I did not like to slow down. I also have a strong stubborn streak, and I always thought that the next time would be different. It was not; it never is. In the moment, I did not like the inconvenience of slowing down to replenish. I just wanted to finish, and slowing down delayed the finish.

> There are more needs in front of us than we can possibly care for.

When caring for others, the truth of the matter is that there are more needs in front of us than we can possibly care for. While we are alive, we will never run out of opportunities to care, and we will never finish caring for people. That is one reason I limit my consumption of media, because media reminds me there are more people out there facing challenges.

Within myself, I only have so much reserve that I can use to care for others until it begins to run low. The same goes for you, which is why one-minute vacations are so valuable. They are vacations along the way that keep us replenished. They keep us from "being out." They can be one tool, among many, that helps us from burning out. They keep us engaged and ready to care for those who cross our paths until we have the opportunity for a more extended amount of time to replenish.

Signs That You Need to Replenish

When I was in ninth grade, my parents installed an in-ground pool in our backyard. The pool has been a great source of joy, fun, and sun for our family for years. But while we were putting the pool in, that sense of joy was absent. It was a lot of work and toil.

I remember the day very well when the machinery arrived to tear out the tree roots and move dirt to make way for the hole for the pool. The excitement was palpable. The men with the machinery dug and dug, and at the end of the day, there was a giant hole that any young boy or girl could be proud of. Amazingly, or surprisingly, when they finished digging, there was a small amount of water in the bottom of the hole. Only eight inches or so. I thought, "Awesome, free water." But I quickly deduced that no one else agreed that this free water was such a good thing.

With the walls of the hole being dirt and not yet cemented in place, the water proved to be a major problem for days and weeks to come. We went to bed the first night and were surprised to discover the next day about 24 inches of water had accumulated in the hole overnight.

I became the grunt labor, and my job was to help pump the water out of the hole. The adults looked and hypothesized about the source of the water; none could be found. The water was clean and could be used, but it was in the wrong place.

Many solutions were tried to divert the water, but it was like Bill Murray in *Groundhog Day*, waking up to the same thing, the same story over and over again.

Ultimately, it was decided that we had an artesian well in our backyard. When the excavator dug the hole, the concealed water came to the surface.

I have often wished for this type of source within me, one that replenished each night without needing to do anything. But that is just not reality. We acknowledge that we are not God and need replenishment and time away. But what are some signals that can alert us that our tank is running low, and we are nearing empty?

If you have ever run out of gas on the interstate or had a car break down after you ignored the strange sounds under the hood, you realize that it is much better to be proactive than reactive.

I wish I could say neither has ever happened to me, but well, they have. Recently, we bought a used car. Both of our kids are learning to drive, and this little car was perfect for learning. I noticed that the car made some noise when it started up. The belts squealed a little and were slightly embarrassing, but once the car was moving, the squealing stopped with no issues until the next morning when the process repeated itself: squealing, embarrassment, wondering what it was.

Until one day the process did not repeat itself. The car broke down in the middle of the busiest intersection in town. The embarrassment was there, but the squealing was not. The little car for learning to drive had given us fair warning, time and time again in fact, that there was something wrong, but I just ignored the noise under the hood, thinking it would work itself out. And it did. It worked itself out. By stopping.

This is so true of our lives as we care for others. Nieuwhof has written widely on the topic of burnout and his own experience with it. While his perspective has been specifically applied for burnout in leaders, I think the common signs he shares are equally applicable to those who are caring for others (whether a leader or not).

Nieuwhof lists several signs that offer clues to know if we are running low.[25] These are the nine things he lists and how I see them applying to a *caring life*:

1. **Your motivation has faded.** The desire and drive you had to care for others are not there anymore. In fact, you begin looking for ways to avoid caring rather than embracing the honor of caring for others.

2. **Your main emotion is "numbness"—you no longer feel the highs or the lows.** Caring for others used to give you a sense of gratitude. You were able to cry with those that were suffering and rejoice with those who were doing well. Now, you have no emotions, and if you do have emotions, you refuse to acknowledge them. You are detached both from the emotions of the person you are caring for and from your own emotions.

3. **People drain you.** Caring for people makes you feel like you are "on" or "performing," and you are tired of being "on" and "performing." So, you seek opportunities where you do not have to be. This is one of the biggest signs for me, when I hear myself saying, "I am tired of being 'on' or 'performing.'" It is a squeaky-belt-on-my-car moment.

4. **Little things make you disproportionately angry.** When you find yourself getting angry at the person you are caring for under trivial circumstances. You have a short fuse, and when your fuse is lit, you assign motives that are less than kind.

5. **You're becoming cynical.** You begin to think that caring for others is a waste of your time, that people are taking advantage of you and your desire to care. You feel you are being used.

6. **Your productivity is dropping.** A warning sign for me is when the creativity or the art of caring is no longer present. I am in trouble when I continually return to the same things I did in the past to care for people with no regard for the person or their challenge because I do not have the energy to be creative.

7. **You're self-medicating.** Replenishing, reenergizing, recharging, and refreshing are necessary when we care for others. How we choose to do these things and their effectiveness in helping us accomplish our goal is another question. When we turn to destructive behaviors to escape, it is a warning sign.

8. **You don't laugh anymore.** You have simply lost your smile and ability to see the joy in life. I know when I watch *Everybody Loves Raymond* and don't crack a smile, I am drained.

9. **Sleep and time off no longer refuel you.** Caring can wear us out. We need downtime. It is common and expected, so when we return from our time of refueling and are more tired than when we started to rest, that is a warning sign.

Did one or more of these resonate with you? Or perhaps they brought another sign to mind that points to you running low. Share those with someone you know and trust. If you are single, a friend or mentor who can help you stay accountable is invaluable. If you are married, that person may be your spouse.

> We need to draw from a source greater and deeper than our own.

I have seen that sometimes we do not hear the truth in love from our spouses. When we are running low, we assign motives to our spouse that are simply not true. When we are not at our healthiest, we are not seeing and thinking clearly as to see their care and concern for what it truly is. So, sometimes we need someone outside the family that we give permission to speak directly and honestly to us. Since they do not live with us, we can go our separate ways once the truth in love has been shared. Whatever you choose, accountability is vital.

DEVELOPING YOUR CARING LIFE

My source for caring for others is based on my love and relationship with Christ. The psalmist wrote, "All my springs are in you" (Psalm 87:7 ESV). Springs provide fresh, clean water. Springs provide nourishment and strength. We need to draw from a source greater and deeper than our own. You may not agree with my beliefs in Jesus, but I do know that we can only go so long pouring out and caring for others before we have nothing left to give. The following questions will help you find the source you draw from to replenish and nourish your soul:

A Fool's Choice

1. What are your thoughts on the "burn out or rust out" idea when it comes to caring?

2. How did you feel with that labeled as a fool's choice?

3. What practices have you put into place to let you know if you are running too fast and furious?

Caring Requires a Source

1. What are some practices that drain you?

2. What do you do to replenish, recharge, reenergize, and refresh?

3. How do you stay connected to the source that fills your tank?

One-Minute Vacations

1. Did the idea of a one-minute vacation resonate with you?

2. Do you think this is something you could practice?

3. How can you remind yourself to take one-minute vacations?

Signs That You Need to Replenish

1. From the list of signs by Carey Nieuwhof, do any resonate with you?

2. Have you experienced any of them?

3. Do you have someone who holds you accountable? If not, are there reasons you avoid this?

CHAPTER 10

A Better Offer

About 20 years ago, we moved to France to study French. It was during the time when the French and the Americans were not getting along, and Americans renamed French fries "freedom fries."

We also found out around that time that Heather was pregnant with our first child. We were so excited, though honestly, I was clueless. We moved to a town in the French Alps, a truly picturesque place. My wife was pregnant with our daughter, but pregnancy did not agree with her. She was so sick for a large part of it.

Our trip there was full of stories of missing flights, deadly heat advisories, and poor attempts at saying the name of the town where we were moving. I will not bore you with all the stories but to say we finally arrived to the town via train and were so excited to move into our new apartment. We were hot and sweaty from the long trip there, and what we wanted to do more than anything was take a shower and get cleaned up.

The gentleman who picked us up was very kind and spoke some English, which was a blessing. He drove us to our new apartment, which itself was beautiful. It was just what we imagined an apartment in France to look like. It overlooked the main street in town with a big church at the end of the road. As the driver dropped us off, he also dropped a key piece of information: The apartment did not yet have water.

Wow. OK. We were jetlagged, hot, and sweaty, and Heather was not feeling well. And there was no water. The man also told us that it was a holiday weekend so it would be a few days before there was water in the apartment.

A river ran past our new apartment, so I thought that maybe, just maybe, I could bring some West Virginia to France and bathe in the river.

But I refrained.

Before he left, he made a common offer that I find myself saying often: "If you need anything, please let me know." Or sometimes I say, "I am here to help with whatever you need whenever you need it. I will do my best to help." Or "I will be praying for you, and if you need anything, do not hesitate to call me." Have you used any similar statements? To be honest, sometimes I mean it and sometimes it rolls off my tongue before I realized what I have just said. But in general, I know when I say these things (or some form of them), my heart and mind are normally in the right place, but do I truly mean "anything you need whenever you need it"?

We are on our way to exploring a better offer to care, but before we head there, I want to discuss some reasons as to why this "whatever you need, do not hesitate to call whenever you need it" is not the best way to state our desire to care for someone else.

Whatever-Whenever Puts the Onus
on the One Receiving Care

When someone is in a challenging time, they often can have so many decisions to make it leaves them feeling overwhelmed and suffering from decision fatigue. The questions they *need* to answer can be ones they never imagined having to answer.

So, even if well-intentioned, which it almost always is, the statement of "call me whenever for whatever you need" is just another decision added to that person's list. When we offer to do whatever and whenever for someone who is directly caring for their loved one, it can also add to their already full plate. Our good intentions to demonstrate that we care can actually drain precious energy and require effort that someone might not have or may not want to expend.

Please hear me. I know it is not your desire or mine to put more decisions on someone else or to ask them to expend the energy they have. I am not passing judgment on you or myself, and this is not an attempt to make anyone feel bad. At the same time, if the person that we desire to show we care is not able to receive our care due to the way it is presented, ultimately, it is a lose-lose situation.

My go-to statement for years has been "call me whenever for whatever you need," but now, rather, I do my best to suggest some things that I can and am willing to do. For instance, I may say: "I want to help during this difficult time, and I like to make meals for other people. I make a killer apple pie and chicken noodle soup. Could I bring it to you this Thursday at 5 p.m.?" I have also started saying something like: "I will be thinking between now and then about other meals I could make, and if you have suggestions, I am open to them if more meals would be of help. I will be in touch in 24 to 48 hours with more ideas."

> **Put intentionality and effort into your offer.**

This opens the door for them to share their preferences with me and also puts the onus on me to get back to them, rather than on them to get back in touch with me.

In this type of statement, you, the care provider, are doing the heavy lifting when it comes to decision-making and communicating. All the other person needs to do is say yes or no. It also shows you have put intentionality and effort into your offer, and I truly believe people feel more cared for when there is intentionality and effort behind our acts of caring.

If they say no, you must promise not to be offended. I mean it. When it comes to caring for others, you must turn your "easily offendable button" to the off position. As my friend Arnold shares, you need to put your big toe away, so others cannot easily step on it. Someone who is hurting can often hurt others and not even know that they have. If your offer of apple pie and chicken noodle soup is ever turned down, call me and I will gladly take them and eat them in that order.

Whatever-Whenever Is *Very* Unclear

People hesitate to ask for anything when we say "whatev-er-whenever" because they do not know what we mean. When something is unclear, it can create anxiety and stress in the very person you are trying to care for. Often, people are concerned that if they make a request that does not fit into your "whatever-whenever" that you will feel obligated, and they will feel embarrassed.

Think about it. Whatever includes a lot of things. Technically, by definition, it includes...everything. I know the sense of what I mean when I say "whatever." It includes the things I feel comfortable asking someone else to help me with. My "whatever" is heavy with my perspective and laden with my biases.

As we saw with expectations and assumptions, our "whatever" is often not the same, and sometimes not even close. I have seen situations in which someone going through a difficult time made a request that to them was a reasonable "whatever," only to have their friend, colleague, leader, or pastor who said "whatever-whenever" give reasons why the request did not fall into "whatever-whenever" and was not possible. If you want to create distance between you and another person, offer "whatever" and then when they ask, proceed to tell them why their "whatever" is unreasonable and unrealistic, and tell them all the reasons you cannot do what they are asking. I guarantee they will be confused and hurt.

And what time does "whenever" occupy? Once again, whenever could mean "at any time" or 24/7, 365 days a year. I say "whenever," but I am not available "whenever." I am available sometimes, but not at all times.

In the past, I said to those I served and cared for: "If you have a medical need, I am available whenever you need me." I received calls at 2 a.m. from those who could not sleep. I received a visit after midnight for a medical condition that had been put off until it was convenient for them, which happened to be 1 a.m. I quickly realized I did not truly mean "whenever." I meant a "whenever" that was logical to me. I thought everyone automatically knew what that time frame was. I was wrong. I proceeded to clarify that my "whenever" really meant from 8 a.m. to 8 p.m. Unless it was for a child, then I truly meant 24/7, 365 days a year.

It is up to us to share what our "whatever-whenever" means. Each individual can help the person they are caring for by making their "whatever-whenever" as clear as possible. If we truly desire to care for others, this will be paramount.

Whatever-Whenever Can Be Seen as Ingenuine

I have listened to pastors and read books that discussed phrases we frequently say without even thinking about what we are saying. We have learned the culturally appropriate response and use it whether we mean it or not. One of the clearest examples is how we greet each other. Most places I have lived and served has some form of "how are you doing today?" As I studied French, More, and Malagasy, I was taught proper responses to the greeting, but I do not remember any of them giving the option of including how you are truly doing. Our greetings have become a pattern heavy on pleasantry but not authenticity.

Over time, I have seen the "whatever-whenever" fall into this category. We know it is the right thing to say and we have learned when to say it. We hear it at work, read it on social media, or often just say it. But just like with our greetings, the authenticity of it can come into question.

Once again, do not get me wrong. I believe there are people reading this book who truly mean it when they say "whatever-whenever." But I have done a not-so-scientific study and found that those who truly mean it are less than one percent of us. This one percent would give you whatever they had, whenever you needed it. It is who they are. But in my experience, they are a zebra among horses. The rest of us, the 99 percent, fall into the more common category of just saying it because it is the right thing to say at the moment.

We know that communication takes at least two people. If the person communicating is responsible to transmit the message, then it is up to the caregiver to communicate that they are being authentic when they offer to care for someone. You may be the zebra, the one percent, but if the person you say it to is in the 99 percent, like me, then they will interpret what you say through their personal lens, which is "he does not really mean whatever-whenever."

∨

Removing ambiguity from your offer to care shows intentionality, forethought, and authenticity.

My challenge for you is the next time you get ready to say "whatever-whenever," pause briefly before it comes out of your mouth. Reflect on whether you are acting authentically and if you truly mean what you are saying. If you don't mean it, just do not say it. Offer to do what you can and provide clarity to that. I think clarifying and removing the ambiguity from your offer to care shows intentionality, forethought, and authenticity, and I believe the person you are desiring to care for will be more apt to receive it.

Some of you have been disagreeing with me for pages. You are the zebras. But I hope the next time you say "whatever-whenever," there will be a little pause as you ask, "Is this really what I mean?"

The Better Offer of Care

The better offer of care shows intentionality, authenticity, and forethought about what you can truly do to care for someone else. The better offer answers the who, what, when, where, and why. It may look different depending on the situation, but here are a few examples:

1. John, I want to help you mow the grass in your yard once a week from now to the end of September as you recover from

your knee replacement. If I could use your mower, I will pay for the gas. This is something I can do to help, and I cannot accept payment. I can start this week. Would you allow me to use my talent to do this for you?

2. Tina, I remember when I had three toddlers at home. Those were great but tiring times. Could I make a meat lasagna and salad for you and your family? I could bring the meal every other Thursday around noon. I love to cook, and this is something I want to do for you over the next six months. I cannot accept payment. Would you allow me to do this for you and your family?

3. Frank, I know you are caring for your wife after her surgery. I would like to buy you a gift card to a restaurant so you can order a few meals and won't have to cook for a few days. I was thinking [restaurant name]. Would you allow me to do this?

4. Tammy, I am sorry that you tore your ACL in practice the other day. I know you love playing high school volleyball. After your surgery, you won't be able to drive to school. Would you allow me to pick you up every morning and take you home after practice until you can drive again?

DEVELOPING YOUR CARING LIFE

A better offer requires intentionality, authenticity, and forethought. I submit a better offer avoids the "whatever-whenever" conundrum and communicates your true desire to care without placing more decisions on someone who already has enough decisions to make. Here are a few questions to get you thinking:

Whatever-Whenever Puts the Onus on the One Receiving Care

1. Do you ever catch yourself saying, "I can help you. Whatever you need, whenever you need it, I am there"?

2. Has someone ever offered "whatever-whenever" to you, and when you mustered the courage to ask, they did not do it?

3. Are you easily offended if someone does not accept your offer to care? If so, what are some reasons you are offended and how can you move towards being less offendable?

Whatever-Whenever Is *Very* Unclear

1. What are some reasons being clear is important when you offer to care for others?

2. What do you really mean when you say, "whatever you need"? Once you can figure this out, it will help you be clearer in your offer.

3. What do you really mean when you say, "whenever you need it"? Once you can figure this out, it will help you be clearer in your offer.

Whatever-Whenever Can Be Seen as Ingenuine

1. Do you really mean "whatever-whenever," or is it something you say out of habit?

2. If you say this out of habit, can you see how this can be viewed as ingenuine?

3. How can you make your offer to care for others more genuine and thought out?

The Better Offer of Care

1. What is your better offer?

2. Does it include who, what, when, where, and why?

3. Will you offer the same offer to everyone, or will you choose certain offers for certain people?

CHAPTER 11

Caring Cross-Culturally

I was once again invited to go to the west coast of Madagascar to provide medical care in some remote villages, some of which had never had outsiders visit. Through my adventures, I have discovered that if someone tells me that outsiders have not yet been to a village or certain region, there is a reason. Either the village is physically hard to access, a language barrier exists, or a village simply does not want visitors from the outside. It can also be a combination of the three (or some other reason entirely), but rest assured there is usually a reason as most of the easier places have already been visited.

Navigating Culture: My Story

My journey to these remote villages involved a small 10-seater airplane, canoes, a hovercraft, and one of the oldest forms of transportation, my own two feet. I was told the plan was to fly on the airplane to a remote grass airstrip, then cross the river in canoes where we would spend the night, and then take the hovercraft upriver the next morning. When I arrived at the airport for the first leg of the journey, I was informed that I would be responsible for and leading the multinational team of 10 people of whom most were complete strangers to me. To say I was surprised that I was the leader was an understatement as I am normally just responsible for the medical team. But this journey would be different.

As I assessed the situation during the flight to the remote runway, I quickly became aware that there could be obvious challenges within the team. One team member noted that there would be some daring water travel required once we landed. The problem was that the doctor I served with did not swim. I asked about life vests which are vital for water safety, but I was told logistics had left them behind in the capital city because of the added weight and space they took on the small plane. So, regrettably, life vests were not on hand for us to use.

The second challenge I noted was the pronounced language barrier amongst us. I noticed that the experienced Malagasy hovercraft pilot did not speak a common language with the inexperienced and in-training European hovercraft pilot. Both pilots were extremely kind and amicable men, but their inability to efficiently and effectively communicate could be a real weakness and could impact us all.

Another challenge that concerned me was our mode of upriver transportation. The logistical team had chosen a hovercraft for the upriver leg of the journey as the river we were traveling on was known for being broad and shallow. This made long upriver travel difficult in most typical boats and canoes, and as I mentioned earlier this difficulty in accessing the villages was one reason they had never been visited. In theory, the hovercraft would glide on top of the water or dry land thus expediting our journey upriver. But we soon found out that theory and reality can be two different things.

As we landed on the remote runway and the doors opened to reveal the balmy heat, my mind was racing. We quickly unloaded our supplies, carried them to the river, and got in canoes to make our way across it. The river was milk chocolate brown in color, very shallow, and about 100 meters wide. The canoes were valuable to help us transport all of our gear, but the canoes were weighed down and kept dragging bottom. We had to get out of the canoes several times to move them into water deep enough for them to float.

On one attempt to move the canoes, I noticed some eyes at water level off in the distance. Pretty convinced it was crocodile, I asked our guide if I was correct. He answered in the affirmative that, yes, many crocodiles were in the water, but we had nothing to worry about because an agreement had been made between the ancestors of the crocodiles and the ancestors of the villagers; the villagers fed the crocodiles and in turn, they did not eat humans. I asked whether outsiders, like myself, were included in their agreement. He thought for a second and responded with a mischievous smile, "Well, maybe you should pay close attention. You were not included in the agreement."

The rain poured that night, and the river went from a shallow, slow, meandering river to a river moving at what could be called "flood stage." The raging water moved swiftly and was almost dark chocolate in color now. Interestingly enough, we saw 40 to 50 cows and three or four young men quickly floating down the river. A sight I will never forget. The villagers noted that this was a common way to move their cattle; the cattle herders drove the cows into the water and floated them downriver to different pastures.

I had been excited to ride in a hovercraft, but that excitement began to dissipate as the realization of riding on this river set in. This was a major challenge. Over the next few hours, the water level dropped dramatically, and the river became noticeably calmer. So, we loaded up into the hovercraft for what promised to be an adventure.

I had not researched hovercrafts, and honestly, if I had, I probably would have convinced myself not to ride on one. But with fewer adventures come fewer stories. As I mentioned, the European pilot of the hovercraft was new to the field and the experienced Malagasy pilot was teaching/guiding/mentoring him. Once we got in the hovercraft the lack of common language between the two of them became pronounced; they could only communicate with each other via gestures. It became evident that the Malagasy pilot knew exactly what he was doing, while the European pilot, who was given the lead role, was struggling at best. Still, the Malagasy pilot never took control of the hovercraft, even though several of us asked him repeatedly to do so. He would not. I had failed to consider how much the cultural barriers would accentuate the language barriers.

As we began, we hit a small house and knocked part of it down. We hit trees, rocks, and pretty much anything else in our way and *not* in our way. With each apology from the pilot our confidence in him dwindled. Meanwhile, the doctor who could not swim was popping his blood pressure pills, literally. He was scared. We were all scared. Each time we hit another object, walking seemed a lot more appealing.

Finally, we made it to a smaller body of water like a creek. As we made our way up the creek, the ride became much calmer. But we saw a sharp turn up ahead, where the water was coming down and hitting a rock face and then shooting 90 degrees in our direction. Our pilot needed to navigate this turn if we were going to make it to our destination. Unfortunately, our hovercraft was not designed for 90-degree turns, and we ran full force into a sandbank, jolting and jerking us all.

As we climbed out of the hovercraft, we noticed a 100 or so villagers watching us. We put on a marvelous show for them as we all pitched in to dig the hovercraft out of the sand before deciding we had had enough riding in the hovercraft and decided to trek the rest of the way.

The villagers accompanied us, guiding us on the path. We came to a small, slow-moving stream, and they advised us to remove our shoes to walk in the mud. The mud was like warm chocolate. As we trudged through the mud, I felt something rub against my legs. I asked the guide about it, and he calmly stated that, yes, boa constrictors like to lay in the warm mud.

I do not like snakes. At all. The guide tried to reassure me they were not poisonous, and when they did bite, it did not hurt that bad. But I was out. I scurried out of the water and up the bank and began walking along the ledge as the others were in the water. But within two minutes, I was swarmed by bees. In my shirt. Down my pants. Everywhere. I began taking my clothes off...and fast. I jumped back into the small stream and noticed I was quite a spectacle.

I told the guide there were tons of bees along the bank. He replied, "That's why the villagers prefer the muddy stream. The bees will get you every time, but the snakes only every so often." Lesson learned. The villagers knew where to walk.

We finally made it to the village where we would provide care and share the message of hope we have in Christ. It was a very sweet time. The villagers were thankful and gracious for our visit and the care that we provided. They gave each of us a chicken as a thank you for our visit. We now had four chickens to return with us.

We knew we had to get back in the hovercraft, though none of us were excited for the return trip. The European pilot shared that he had devised a solution to help us navigate the 90-degree turn. He had calculated the distance to the rock face and measured a rope that he would tie one end to a tree and the other to the front of the hovercraft. His thought was that the rope would tighten and swing us around before we ran into the rock face.

It sounded like a great plan, but I could tell the Malagasy pilot was not convinced. Once again, he did not feel like he could share. We prayed and got into the hovercraft. Everything went well at first, as oftentimes things do go well in the beginning. But as we drew closer to the rock face, the water that was rushing behind us and pushing the hovercraft became stronger and faster. The relied-upon rope did not catch and swing us around as planned, and before we knew it, we were jammed between the rock face and the raging water.

The hovercraft began to fill with water as attempts were made to cut the rope. The engine had taken on water and could not be restarted. We had no other choice but to abandon the hovercraft; it was that or be trapped in it. I held onto my non-swimming doctor friend, and we jumped out of the hovercraft together into the water, which swiftly pulled us away from the rock face and deposited us about a 100 meters down the creek on its bank. Soaking wet and shaken, all of us made it except the chickens. The chickens were lost somewhere in the shuffle.

That was the last time I ever traveled in a hovercraft. I am not against them. I now just prefer any form of transportation other than a hovercraft.

Reflection

Sometimes caring for someone who comes from a different cultural background than you can be like the bumpy ride and adventure I had on the hovercraft—full of great intentions, misunderstandings, and miscommunications. It seems like you are together and relating, but you are not really, and despite the good intentions, the caring experience can become painful and traumatic for all involved.

∨

In certain situations, there is someone who knows how to care in a more culturally appropriate way.

In certain situations, there is someone who knows how to care in a more culturally appropriate way. The Malagasy hovercraft pilot knew how to pilot the hovercraft but did not feel that it was culturally acceptable to ask for control of the hovercraft from the European pilot. The person who knows how to care in a more culturally appropriate way may feel it is not acceptable to share what they know unless they are asked to do so. I have found that people frequently want to share but those responsible to ask fail to do so. The European pilot never asked him to take over control of the hovercraft.

Learning to ask someone for cultural advice and counsel takes courage, humility, and self-awareness. Often if we do not ask, those who know will not give advice which further emphasizes the idea that unsolicited advice is often seen as criticism and infrequently heeded. As caregivers, we need to have the courage to ask for cultural guidance. We all need cultural mentors and coaches who we can ask for advice and then follow through with what they suggest.

I have also found that, contrary to common logic, some of the trickier cultural navigation in caring can happen with those who come from the same country and speak the same language as you. A different language and a different home country are strong clues that someone will have differences in how they desire to be cared for.

When someone is from the same country and speaks the same language, we can be fooled into thinking that their family background and culture is the same as ours, and when we use those cultural assumptions to care for someone else, we can quickly realize our assumptions and conclusions were incorrect.

Cultural Understanding

In past decades, if you were born in a rural area such as I was, you would have had to travel the world or to a major metropolitan area in order to see different cultures and ways of living. Cultural understanding was for people who served in the Peace Corps or for international businesses, the military, anthropologists, adventurers, and missionaries.

But as faces continue to change within different nations, new cultural understandings and ways of doing life may be demonstrated by our next-door neighbor, the person sitting beside us at church, our colleague at work, a teammate on our sports team, or perhaps even the doctor who treats us at the hospital.

The differences in culture of those we casually come in contact with can be made more prominent when we desire to care for someone from a different culture than ours.

Dr. Sherwood Lingenfelter shares that culture is the conceptual design, the definitions by which people order their lives, interpret their experiences, and evaluate the behavior of others. He says that culture is the sum of the distinctive characteristics of someone's life.[26] Culture impacts our worldview, our family life, friendships, and many other relationships.

So, if we truly desire to care for someone, we must explore our cultural differences. And if you are really up for learning, dig deeper into Lingenfelter and consider the tensions of time, judgment, crises, goals, self-worth, and vulnerability that he describes. As you investigate these tensions, you realize how misunderstandings in any one of these can hinder us as we attempt to care more effectively cross-culturally.

The Cultural Onion Model

I am a visual learner, so Geert Hofstede's model of culture is helpful to me. Hofstede was a social psychologist dedicated to the study and importance of culture and how different cultures interact. He developed the famous Cultural Onion model which gives a visual representation demonstrating how culture has many layers (see the illustration on the next page).[27] In order to understand a culture, one must peel back the layers.

Hofstede described the layers of culture as symbols, heroes, rituals, practices, and values.

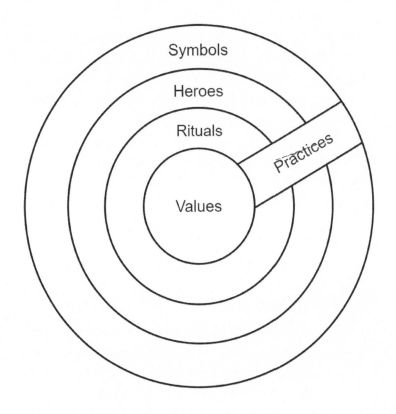

Symbols

The outer layer is symbols, or the visible signs that even someone not from the culture can see. For instance, in my journey
in the hovercraft, there were obvious signs that the two pilots
had different cultural symbols. One of the most evident ones
was the difference in language. It was noticeable to us all. Another cultural symbol was communication style of the indirect
Malagasy and the direct European. But even with these evident
symbols, cultural blindness prevailed because they did not take
time to reflect on the obvious cultural differences.

Another example of symbols was the clothing of the chief whose village we were visiting. He was dressed in clothes different than the rest of the villagers, and his clothing was very different than mine and the rest of the multinational team. The wooden pole in the middle of the village with a zebu head at the top of it was another obvious cultural symbol. It was a symbol of ancestral worship visible to all who entered the village and a clear reminder to the team that the culture of the village was different than ours.

If you live in the West, your neighbor is not likely to have zebu head in the front yard. Instead, one might see images of the Eiffel Tower for France or the Statue of Liberty for the United States. Where I grew up, hex signs (folk art) on barns and homes were common in Pennsylvania Dutch country. Other symbols could be a Buddha statue in someone's home or a cross around someone's neck. All of these give some idea of a person's cultural, religious, or national background.

Heroes

The next layer in Hofstede's Cultural Onion is the heroes of the culture. One good way to understand what a culture values and aspires to is to look at its heroes. Where I grew up, athletes were the town heroes, specifically football players. My first few years of university study were in a school that also looked up to athletes, after which I transferred to another school where the artists were the heroes. Heroes often portray cultural ideals, whether attainable or not, and are a valuable insight into what is important to someone you desire to care for.

When I was growing up, independent people and those who could pull themselves up by the bootstraps were considered heroes. If you were able to overcome insurmountable odds on your own with seemingly little to no assistance from someone else, you were written about and looked up to. This mentality dramatically impacts how someone asks for or accepts care. If we truly desire to care for someone who holds this independent hero mindset, then we need to be creative. If not, our care will end up making them feel like they are less than.

I have a particularly humorous story from my childhood that gives a good example here. Growing up, my family went to church every Sunday morning, Sunday evening, and Wednesday evening. No questions asked. There was no negotiation, and no decision was needed because we were going. This meant we drove by Dairy Queen and several other restaurants at least six times a week. My dad provided well for our family, but there was not enough money to stop at restaurants as frequently as Americans do today. That did not stop me from asking if we could stop at Dairy Queen whenever we passed it, even though the law of averages told me the answer was mostly going to be "no."

One Sunday on the way to church, I asked about stopping at the restaurant after church. The response was that we did not have the money to go out to eat and we were going home for lunch.

Well, I went to Sunday School and asked for prayer.

Maybe you can see where this is going.

In class I asked for prayer because my family was poor and did not have any money. The Sunday School teachers led us in prayer and prayed for the Santmyire family who was going through a tough time and did not have any money.

God did not answer my prayer. We went home for lunch, and I honestly did not think anything more about my request.

We were true Pentecostals and in those days, that meant a nap between morning and evening service. For me it was a forced nap; I had too much energy for this.

But midway through that particular Sunday afternoon, there was a knock at the front door. That was odd. My mom answered the door, and I heard the voice of my Sunday School teacher. She had brought some bags of groceries for our family to help us in our time of need. My mom was surprised and had no idea what this was about. She tried to explain that my dad was not furloughed and that we had plenty of food to eat. My teacher, knowing that our community looked up to those who pulled themselves up by the bootstraps, did not accept my mom's explanation.

I was called to the living room and immediately knew I was in trouble. Big trouble. I tried to backtrack, but that rarely works. I explained to my Sunday School teacher that I had maybe, kinda, not told the truth. But even then, she was not convinced. My mother had to show her the food in our cabinets and the leftovers from lunch we had eaten just a few hours earlier.

Understanding cultural heroes and the reasons we look up to them is vital in providing care. If not, we can unintentionally bring a feeling of shame in the midst of another's difficult circumstances. This is the reason the Malagasy pilot never asked to take control of the hovercraft. In his culture, asking would have brought shame on his European counterpart, and bringing shame on someone else is to be avoided.

Rituals

Rituals are the next layer of the Cultural Onion. These are the things we do out of habit. There is very little thought that goes into them; rituals are just what we do. For years on Friday evenings, our family has eaten pizza and watched a movie. We do not put much thought into the planning. It's just what we do. Some people begin the day drinking coffee, while others read a book before bedtime.

In Madagascar, one of the most important rituals, whether in the city or countryside, was male circumcision. In the villages, young boys around age three were prepared for this particular ceremony. On the day of circumcision, the boys were lined up and a specially appointed person from the village used a knife to perform a freehanded circumcise on each of them. Doing circumcisions without anesthetic was a true act of courage for these young boys, but commonly, they never made very much noise. There was little crying. The days that followed were uncomfortable though, and it was common to see the boys wearing a kilt-looking garment and waddling from here to there.

Now, if that part of the ritual made you grimace, the next part might be worse because the next part of the circumcision ritual was even more challenging for an outsider to understand. After the circumcision, a banana was peeled and prepared, and the foreskin of the grandson was placed on the banana for the grandfather to eat. This ritual provided formal acceptance of the grandson into the family. Extremely hard for an outsider to understand, but for the Malagasy in the village, this is "the way it is and how we do circumcisions."

Values

In the middle of the Cultural Onion are the cultural values and assumptions. As easy as cultural symbols are for most to see and identify, cultural values and assumptions are the opposite. They can be difficult to understand. Cultural values are some of the first things children learn, though as they grow and develop, they might not even be aware of or recognize them. These values are connected to the earlier conversation about unconscious expectations. Many of our unconscious expectations are linked to lessons we learned as young children. Our cultural values are the "why" behind what we do.

Cultural Dissonance

One last story. My friend Jay and I traveled to the southern part of the island to a town that neither of us had ever visited. We were excited to visit the pastor who was living in the community to encourage him and his family. When we arrived, it was evident that this place was like no other we had ever been.

We began to set up the medical clinic, but before we knew it, there was utter chaos. There was pushing and shoving, and no semblance of order. It was a tough beginning to our trip. We decided to put the medical clinic on hold and to find somewhere to sleep for the night. We were told of a "really nice" place in the middle of town; several small, thatched-roof huts served as sleeping quarters for travelers like us. The huts were on the main road, literally—one could stick their finger through the thatch and touch anyone walking by.

That afternoon we heard a generator start up and music began to play. The guitar player had about as much expertise in playing the guitar as I had in playing the piano, trumpet, or tuba. He knew one tune, and he played that tune from 3 p.m. that afternoon until the next morning. He played the tune so many times, I can still replay it in my head like it was just this morning.

After dinner, we called it a day and returned to our hut on the main road. Jay and I normally stay in the same room for accountability purposes, and this night was no different. We both eventually fell asleep but were awakened at midnight with gunfire right outside our "luxury" accommodations. Seven shots in succession. I was sure this was it and they were coming after us. Jay and I jumped out of the bed, checked for bullet holes, discovered there were none, and started to laugh (it was one of those laugh or cry situations).

The gunfire outside the hut continued all night long. Every hour on the hour, seven shots were fired. Sleep was not something we experienced much that evening. We were ready for morning to come.

Early morning arrived and the guitarist stopped playing his music, which coincided with the start of a march through town. We asked around and learned that the festivities of the night were the result of a town elder dying. We watched as his body was placed in an ox cart and two young men began to pull the ox cart by putting their heads through the yokes and pulling as hard as they could. People lined the dirt road and cheered and sang and shouted. Slowly but surely, the young men made progress, pulling the ox cart towards the edge of town while onlookers poured *tok-gasy* (homemade moonshine) down their open mouths.

At the edge of town were 200 or more cattle lying dead in the hot sun. It was like a cattle massacre. We were told that when a person died, the custom was to slaughter all of their cattle in order for the cattle to go with them to the afterlife. The value of these people was not focused here on earth; their cultural value was focused on the afterlife.

Learning from Lepers

Your story of caring cross-culturally may look different than many of mine, which is to be expected. Each of us are in unique situations and seasons of life. At the same time, there are some common keys or mindsets that will help anyone who desires to care cross-culturally. They come from a story in the Bible that I had to read over and over again before it sank in.

The story is in 2 Kings chapter 7. If you know the story of the four lepers well, you can skip the next few paragraphs. If not, read on for a great story that offers three keys to caring cross-culturally. If you do not believe in the Bible and the stories it contains, this story still has a lot to offer you. Allow me to paraphrase what Andy Stanley says: We frequently read and consume content we don't believe in.

This story recounts the ordeal of four lepers who sat outside the city gates during a siege that had led to a famine. In those days, people with leprosy were not allowed into the city limits due to fears that they would spread their skin disease to others. (Quarantine is not a modern idea.)

The lepers could not work in the city and therefore could not purchase food, making them reliant on others. They stayed outside the city and depended on those inside to give them food. But it was a time of famine. When a parent does not have food for their own family due to famine, they cannot give elsewhere. You cannot give what you do not have. The lepers received nothing because those in the city had nothing to give.

The lepers realized that if they stayed at the city gates, they would likely starve to death. So, they decided to go down to the enemy's camp and surrender. They figured that if enemy was hostile and killed them, it was better than sitting still and waiting to die. If the enemy accepted them and gave them food, great! And if they did not, they were going to die anyway. The text reads that they had nothing to lose.

They proceeded down to the enemy's camp only to find that the enemy had abandoned their camp and left everything behind. Gold, silver, food, and clothes were all there for their taking. The lepers had hit the jackpot, so to speak. After they had taken for themselves, they had a decision to make: Were they going to care for those in the city who were starving and tell them about what they had found, or were they going to keep it to themselves?

Ultimately, they went back to the city and told the people what they had found. The king was not convinced that what they experienced was true. He was concerned that the enemy had set a trap, and when the people went down to partake, they would be attacked and overrun by the enemy. But the lepers were correct. The information they shared was true, and their act of sharing and caring with those in the city saved the city from starvation.

Those who believe in the Bible recognize that God ran the enemy army off. God provided the solution, and His solution was to use the lepers to share the good news.

Now, you may be asking, "Great story, Aaron, but what does it have to do with caring cross-culturally? What characteristics of these lepers apply to me and my desire to care cross-culturally?" Glad you asked.

Three Keys to Caring Cross-Culturally

The first key to caring cross-culturally is resisting complacency. The lepers could have easily sat at the gate, accepted the situation as it was, and done nothing. The apathy (indifference) that comes with complacency (self-satisfaction) is one of the biggest enemies of caring cross-culturally.

Caring cross-culturally can be uncomfortable. It can feel awkward at first. If you are looking for the easiest thing to do, caring cross-culturally will not top the easy list. It is hard. It can be complex. It takes time, energy, and prayer.

If you desire to care cross-culturally, you must work at being a person that resists complacency. Caring cross-culturally requires action and movement. It requires resiliency and means not giving up or giving in.

> To care cross-culturally, you must have courage.

I encourage you to start slow and build off of your wins. Not all of your attempts to care cross-culturally will be wins but celebrate the ones that are. Use those wins as inspiration to continue forward.

The second characteristic the lepers displayed is courage. It took great courage for them to go down to the enemy's camp to surrender to them. If you have had an enemy, you know the amount of courage it takes to put your life in their hands. I am not suggesting that people run out and put their lives in their enemy's hands, but I am saying that to care cross-culturally, you must have courage. Courage is paramount.

Often, this is the struggle that hinders us from caring cross-culturally today. Many of us do not begin caring from a place of courage, but rather from a place of fear. The close cous-in to complacency (the big enemy) and apathy is fear. It will be challenging, at best, to care for someone from another culture, another worldview, and another perspective in life if paralyzed by fear.

I have tried finding courage in many things—more education, more understanding, more cultural insight, better language capability, and cultural guides. All have been valuable, while at the same time not enough to dispel my fears. The only thing I have found that has provided true courage is my relationship with Jesus. To care cross-culturally you must have courage.

The last characteristic demonstrated by the lepers was a high tolerance for criticism. The lepers shared great news for the city, but the king was suspicious: Were they seeing the situation correctly? Or was this a trap from the enemy? What we do not read in the story is the lepers trying to convince the king that they are right and that the news they have shared is correct.

Those who care cross-culturally must have a high tolerance for questions, doubts, and suspicions. Their motives may be questioned and doubted, and people may be suspicious of them.

I cannot count how many times this has happened to me— from the woman in a rural area chewing me out for holding a clinic in the village with the intention of stealing the teenage girls, or the Chinese businessman living in another town where we conducted a medical clinic accusing me of being a CIA spy. I had a genuine desire to care for others who did not look like me, live like me, act like me, or see the world as I saw it, only for that care to get lost in the cultural differences between myself and them. In the beginning, I was often offended and frustrated, but over time, I realized that my reactions were often heavily grounded in my past experience. This applied to both myself and the person I was caring for.

Leadership consultant and author T. J. Addington says that living a life with nothing to prove and nothing to lose is extreme-ly valuable.[27] This has become my go-to phrase when my motives are questioned or when someone is suspicious of me. I simply say to myself, "I have nothing to prove and nothing to lose." It has been so freeing for me to care for others with this mentality. My main struggle was that I wanted to control outcomes and when the outcomes were not what I wanted, I was frustrated. When I let go of controlling and took on the "nothing to prove or lose" mentality, caring cross-culturally was more pure and rich, and less baffling.

If you desire to care cross-culturally, resisting complacency, being of great courage, and having a "nothing to prove, nothing to lose" attitude is a great foundation from which to build. The characteristics of being flexible, adaptable, humble, and many others can be built on the foundation of these three.

DEVELOPING YOUR CARING LIFE

As we care for others from different cultural backgrounds, even if we look similar and speak the same language, we must give time to ponder cultural symbols, rituals, and values. We can integrate the characteristics of resisting complacency, being courageous, and having a high tolerance for suspicion into how we care. If we fail to integrate cultural understanding into our plan, our heartfelt care can be interpreted in many different ways. The following questions will help you further process your journey on caring cross-culturally:

Cultural Understanding

1. What is your definition of culture?

2. How does your culture view caring for others within your cultural group and outside of your group?

3. Do you find it difficult to navigate or understand different cultures? How does that affect your desire and ability to care for others?

The Cultural Onion Model

1. How can your understanding of cultural symbols impact how you care for others?

2. Who are your heroes? What makes them a hero to you? How do these heroes influence how you care for others?

3. What are your core values and how can these core values help or hinder as you care cross-culturally?

Three Keys to Caring Cross-Culturally

1. Is complacency something you struggle with when it comes to caring cross-culturally?

2. Where do you find your courage to care for others who do not have the same worldview?

3. How can you grow in your ability to not be easily offended when your motives are questioned as you care cross-culturally?

CHAPTER 12

An Innovative Culture of Caring

When my son was young and still in a car seat, he loved to take rides in the car. Well, maybe *loved* is a strong word, but it was an outing dad could handle. We had a Toyota Land Cruiser, and I would strap him in, and we'd go for a drive.

Traveling on roads in developing countries is more exciting for both the driver and the passengers than in developed countries. Madagascar is no different. Drivers have many things to dodge and passengers have all kinds of exciting things to see. Although I prefer the orderly roads of the United States, my kids comment on how boring car rides are in the U.S. as they see no real signs of life on the sides of the road.

Because in Madagascar, life is all around.

When we traveled, Josiah sat in the back seat and took in all that life: the zebu carts; the fruit, vegetable, and meat vendors; one-person bikes somehow carrying perilously balanced families of four; trucks loaded with foam mattresses 15-feet high; thirty chickens dangling upside down on the back of a motorcycle; or pigs lying sideways tied down in a push cart. It was never boring.

One evening our family needed some groceries, so I put Josiah in his seat, and off we went. It was a short drive that we knew by heart, but halfway to the store, three men ran out into the middle of the road. In an instant, I had to choose to run them over or to stop. It sounds like an easy decision, but I had no idea what they wanted, though I could tell they were not stopping me to give me a free pineapple.

I stopped.

One of the men approached my window and began yelling something while the other two guys jumped in the car with us, one in the front beside me and the other in the back with Josiah. I know, I should have locked the doors, but they were manual locks. I had mine and Josiah's locked but not the other side.

It all happened in a matter of seconds. The guys in the car yelled at me to drive and chase down a supposed thief. I had no idea what they were talking about, and besides I am a grandpa driver, not a thief chaser. For several seconds, I was in overload. I was taking in information and trying to make a decision. What do I do with this information in front of me? Screaming men. In my car. My son in the back, strapped in his car seat.

The seconds of overload passed, and I made a quick decision. I turned off the car, removed the keys from the ignition, and climbed into the back seat with my son. I took him out of his car seat and got out of the vehicle. As we stood on the side of the road, the men continued to yell at me, insisting that I needed to help them chase the thief. But my West Virginia hardheadedness kicked in. I wanted no part of it. I stood on the side of the road, gripping my son in my arms, not sure what would happen next. Fortunately, someone they knew arrived and they sped away in his car. I never saw them again.

Change Agent

Looking back, I wish I had had a plan. Something pre-determined and well-thought-out, so I would have known what to do and what to expect when those guys jumped in the car with us. Maybe even prevented the whole scenario. (Eventually, we did go through security training to help us develop a plan.)

After reading all of these pages, maybe you are in a state of overload like I was on the road that evening. I had a lot of information to process in a compressed amount of time, and now you are beginning to process how you desire to care for people around you. You want to care for people and probably want to see a broader cultural shift happen in how we provide that care. Hopefully, you are inspired to be a change agent to bring about transformation in the caring culture of your family, your organization, or your community.

Having a guiding theory to help us begin this endeavor of cultural change is paramount. Without one, it will be challenging to stay the course. It can be difficult to know if what we are experiencing is common or if we are missing something, and a theory gives us a plan and path forward. It provides consistency and stability. I want to share a cultural change theory, developed by Dr. Everett Rogers, that I have used when working towards a cultural change. I trust you will find it as valuable as I have as we endeavor to change the culture around how we care for each other.

Change

Before we jump into the change theory (which I have found beneficial as I look to influence how we care for those around us), I

Leading change can be a joyous experience—it can also be a painful one.

must offer a word of caution. Leading change can be a joyous experience—it can also be a painful one.

My grandfather had a farm in Old-town, Maryland. He was primarily a chicken farmer, but he also had bees. The bees were beneficial for producing honey and helping to pollinate the fruit trees on the farm. My dad often quoted my grandfather: "Bees can make you honey or sting you to death. The outcome is largely based on how you treat them."

Each fall, a truck rolled into my grandfather's farm and loaded up the bees to transport them to Florida where they stayed for the winter to pollinate trees and plants there. They were then brought back to the farm in the spring.

My grandfather cautioned the driver that there was a shorter way out of the farm over a bumpy road. It was a time saver, but when the truck arrived in Florida, the bees would be angry and removing them from the truck would be difficult. The stress placed on the bee colony from the bumpy road could also cause some valuable bees to die off. The choice was the truck driver's: to make speed with angry bees or to go slow with happy bees.

My grandfather never knew which road the driver took on the journey to Florida. However, when the truck driver returned the bees to my grandfather's farm, he knew exactly which road the truck driver had chosen on the return trip. If the bees were angry and some had died during the journey, he knew the shorter bumpy road was chosen. If the bees did not seem to know any difference in their travels, he knew the longer, smoother route was chosen. As my grandfather said, bees will make you honey or can sting you to death. It all depends on how you treat them in changing their environment.

People are not bees, but the lesson applies as you lead change. How you care for people during change can make a huge difference on the impact made—both on you as the leader and those you serve.

Change Theory

Everett Rogers developed the theory of Diffusion of Innovations to explain and describe social change.[28] (I include his overarching ideas along with my experiences using them in the discussion that follows.)

In early investigations, Rogers studied the diffusion of agricultural innovations and specifically why some farmers adopted new technologies and advancements, and others did not. He sought to explain the why, how, and speed or rate at which new ideas and practices were spread across the agricultural community. To advance the theory, he tested it cross-culturally and confirmed that the theory was applicable in other cultural settings and was not unique to the United States. Rogers continued drawing conclusions and identified regularities concerning diffusion found across cultures, innovations, and the social groups that adopt innovations.

He identified four main elements of the diffusion process: innovation, communication channels, time, and social systems:

1. Innovation: An idea, practice, or object that is perceived as new by an individual

2. Communication channels: How individuals or groups relay information for the purpose of reaching a mutual understanding

3. Time: A system of measurement that quantifies the rate of passing through an innovation process and the speed of adoption

4. Social system: A set of interrelated units that are involved in joint problem solving to accomplish a goal

The innovation of caring that you will be championing is focused on caring for people in an intentional and dignified way. Dr. Cal Newport discusses how innovation is taking developments from one field and applying them to another. That is exactly what happens when we take these principles and practices of caring for others and integrate them into the marketplace, home, and community. The idea of care is not innovative, but the way we care for others will be seen as an innovation.

> **The idea of care is not innovative, but the way we care for others will be seen as an innovation.**

We talked about the importance of communication in care. I challenge you to consider and develop a plan on how you will communicate as you focus on influencing a caring culture: who you will communicate with, what method of communication you will use, when you will communicate, how you will receive feedback, and how you will measure your effectiveness in communicating a brighter future in how we care for each other. Answers to these statements will be pivotal as you lead a cultural innovation of caring.

The element of time is integral to any cultural change. Realistic time expectations will be valuable for your mental health: At what point in the future will you measure whether the innovation of caring culture is taking hold? Will you measure effectiveness more than once in the future? How will you communicate the importance of measurement?

The element of social systems will also guide how you interact and champion the innovation of caring. Whatever organization, community, or family culture you desire to influence will have different levels of perceived and real standing, authority, and hierarchy. The question of whether those around you will accept this innovation of caring from someone who is or is not in hierarchical leadership will be important and may affect how quickly an innovation of caring will be adopted. Therefore, having cultural champions for the innovation of caring is paramount. Champions should be sought out for their expertise, insight, direction, guidance, understanding, and influence.

Stages of Adoption

Rogers expands on the elements of the diffusion process by delineating five stages that occur in the adoption process of innovation. These five stages are knowledge, persuasion, decision, implementation, and confirmation.

1. Knowledge: An individual becomes aware of an innovation and how it functions. The three stages of knowledge are awareness, application, and principle.

2. Persuasion: An individual forms a perception or attitude towards the innovation regardless of whether it is positive or negative.

3. Decision: An individual decides to accept or reject an innovation.

4. Implementation: An individual decides to put an innovation into practice.

5. Confirmation: An individual seeks affirmation or reinforcement concerning the innovation.

Knowledge of the innovation of caring can be further broken down into awareness knowledge, application knowledge, and principle knowledge. Awareness knowledge comes as you communicate the innovation of caring and the brighter future of a caring innovation in which people belong, matter, are known, and valued for their inherent dignity. As you communicate this vision for the future, you can help move people from awareness knowledge of the innovation of caring to application knowledge, which is necessary to put the caring innovation into action. From application knowledge, adopters of the innovation of caring can further increase their knowledge by understanding information about the principles of how the innovation works.

Persuasion can occur at varying times depending on who you are communicating with and the trust they have in you. Persuasion may occur at the moment you share the innovation of caring, shortly after, or in the days that follow. This is where the value of champions comes in again. Champions with principle and application knowledge of the innovation can provide insight and direction for you. Their support helps persuade others to consider the innovation of caring. It is common for those you communicate with to consider the opinion of their peers before adopting an innovation.

The decision to accept or reject the innovation of caring can also occur at any time after you share it with someone. Factors that could affect this decision are presentation style, perceived need, leadership acceptance, champion's support, local contextual cultural barriers, present challenges, and past experiences with care. I have no skill in marketing or persuading others to accept an innovation. Maybe you do. I caution you to consider the heart behind the innovation of caring and not make it a pressured sell.

Implementation of the innovation of caring by those in the community, family, or place of employment can occur at any time following the awareness of the innovation. If someone decides to implement the innovation of caring, the implementation occurs when the people take the opportunity to care for others in a way that the one they are caring for feels seen, known, valued, and dignified. Examples of this are when someone utilizes the decision-making tool, clarifies expectations and assumptions, or presents a better offer.

In the confirmation stage, those in the community, business, or family seek affirmation from others concerning the innovation of caring. This affirmation can come from a multiplicity of different sources. Confirmation is paramount for the long-term sustainability of any innovation, and the innovation of caring is no different. If confirmation is consistent and positive, the probability of the innovation of caring being successful will dramatically increase.

Stages of Acceptance

Recognizing there are variables that affect the rapidity of acceptance of an innovation, Rogers continued his theory by identifying five variables that influence acceptance.

1. Relative advantage: The improvement of the innovation in comparison with the current model.

2. Compatibility: The relationship of the innovation with the existing values, past experiences, and needs of those who potentially would adopt the innovation.

3. Complexity: The perception of the difficulty to comprehend and implement the innovation.

4. Trialability: The length of commitment needed to experiment with the innovation.

5. Observability: The extent to which the results of the innovation are visible to others.

These five variables will be important for the implementation of the innovation of caring and will influence the rate of adoption.

1. Community and family members, colleagues, and leaders will need to consider the relative advantage or the improvement of the innovation of caring in comparison to their current practice.

2. They will be affected by their relationship and experiences with caring and the common barriers of complexity, past hurt, difficulty in seeing results, inattentiveness to the needs of those around them, and their confidence, or lack thereof, in the innovation.

3. Individuals will need to assess the perceived complexity of understanding and implementing the caring innovation. This could affect the rate of adoption.

4. Community and family members, colleagues, and leaders will need to consider the variable of trialability and its impact on the innovation of caring. Trialability should not inhibit the rate of adoption due to the plethora of opportunities to care for others.

5. Those who observe the innovation will influence and impact those who have adopted the innovation. Team members,

family, members of the community, and other colleagues will also observe changes.

Adopters

Finally, Rogers identified different types of adopters of innovations. He categorized these adopters into five groups: innovators, early adopters, early majority, later majority, and laggards.

1. Innovators: The first to adopt an innovation; risk-takers

2. Early adopters: Discrete and judicious when adopting innovations

3. Early Majority: Take a significant amount of time to adopt an innovation

4. Later Majority: Skeptical about innovations and wait for the majority to adopt them before doing so

5. Laggards: Focused on tradition and have an aversion to change

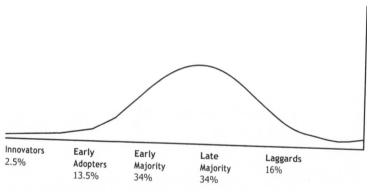

It is vitally important for someone who desires to see a cultural change to recognize that research has proven that change

takes time and follows a predictable curve (see graph on previous page). Immediate 100 percent participation is unrealistic. In my experience, it is realistic to target all categories of adopters but focus on innovators, early adopters, and the early majority. Laggards may not adopt any innovation, let alone an innovation as specific as caring. Therefore, focusing on this subset in the beginning can produce frustration, irritation, and discouragement.

DEVELOPING YOUR CARING LIFE

Whether you decide to use the theory of Diffusion of Innovations as a guide while you lead an innovation of caring is ultimately up to you. I do believe that a change theory as a guide will be invaluable for you both in the near and long term. This theory will guide, strengthen, and give structure to this transformation. The following questions will help you further process the innovation of caring:

Change Agent

1. Have you ever led a cultural change?

2. If you have, what lessons did you learn?

3. If not, what are some reasons you have not engaged in changing culture?

Change Theory

1. What are some key concepts from the change theory that sound interesting to you?

2. What were some areas that were unclear? Did you struggle to understand why they were important?

Stages of Acceptance

1. How can the complexity of caring impact acceptance of changing how you care for others?

2. How important is feedback from observers on whether an innovation of caring is adopted long term?

3. Are you driven by seeking affirmation? How could that impact you?

Adopters

1. Do you consider yourself an innovator?

2. How does focusing on laggards breed discouragement?

3. Who would you focus on as you impact culture with an innovation of caring?

Conclusion

Congratulations! You survived my stories and are still reading! The idea behind *A Caring Life* is paramount for our world today. Even as we advance in the development of technology that simplifies our lives and frees up our time, we often fail to use that extra time to care for those who are more meaningful than things. We have made great advances in time management, vision casting, marketing, strategic engagement, and organizational or business growth. Maybe we drift towards those areas because they are easier.

Borrowing from Einstein, perhaps caring, like politics, is more complicated than nuclear physics, and we just don't know where to begin.

Caring impacts trajectory. Caring for each other helps restore dignity, a word we do not hear much about these days. When we provide care, people feel seen, known, and heard, and even though the impact we have on those we care for is hard to quantify or measure, we do know that caring impacts not only the current generation but also generations to come. Caring for others makes our world larger, taking it from a "me-centered" world to developing relationships that help us realize there is so much more to life than satisfying our desires.

The art of caring. Like any activity that requires creativity, action, and effort, caring is a true art form. Some people are naturally gifted as caregivers and some of us need to acquire the ability, but we can all care for each other. When we acknowledge that caring is an art form, it becomes evident that it is not an input-output correlation. Like art, the outcomes from caring are not guaranteed or universally appreciated by all, but that does not decrease the value and importance of caring.

Common barriers to care. Our fast-paced world can accentuate distractions and augment our inattentiveness to those around us and the challenges they face. When we stop and take in the barrage of media, we can be overwhelmed with the breadth, depth, and magnitude of those who are hurting in our world today. Anyone who has cared knows that at times, caregivers can be hurt by those they are caring for, and this, too, becomes a barrier to ever wanting to care again. Lastly, we discussed the ever-increasing complexity of our world and how complexity can make us hesitant to care.

Caring and self-awareness. The Enneagram and our personal tendencies can affect how we give and receive care. It is one of many valuable tools that can help us be more intentional in how we provide care so that our acts of caring are effective. Caregivers can often drift to providing care in the way they desire to be cared for, but by using a tool like the Enneagram to guide us, we can avoid this common pitfall.

Expectations and assumptions. We each bring expectations and assumptions into how we care for others. Much of the hurt, frustration, and irritation that both the caregiver and the care receiver experience is due to unmet expectations and inaccurate assumptions. If we can explore unconscious, unspoken, not-agreed-upon, and unrealistic expectations, it will be valuable in providing quality care and decreasing frustration and pain.

Communication in care. We can spend vast amounts of time planning to care while forgetting the importance of communication in care. We have so many methods of communication to choose from that we often give into decision fatigue and either communicate in the simplest way or not at all. This is a mistake that would be valuable for all of us to avoid. Being intentional in how we communicate can be as equally important as the act of caring.

Responses to care. To effectively care for others, it is paramount that we notice and consider how those we are caring for respond to our care. Common responses to care include fear, apathy, confidence, and trust. In an ideal world, everyone would have confidence and trust in us as caregivers. But at times, fear and apathy reign supreme. Understanding and awareness of the different types of responses to care will help you better provide care and not be caught off guard when the response you receive is not the one you expected.

Caring in leadership. Leaders shape the culture of caring for those they serve, and the language leaders use to describe how they care for those they serve is vitally important. Leaders do not want to make those they serve feel like commodities, but this can easily happen when using possessive pronouns and organizational management lingo to describe those they serve. Ultimately, with leadership comes authority and great responsibility, and if organizational culture is not caring, the leader holds the responsibility to change it.

Source of caring. The act of caring is pouring oneself out and giving to others what one has. We saw the importance of recharging, replenishing, reenergizing, and refreshing in the life of the caregiver. Caregivers cannot give into the fool's choice of rusting out or burning out; they must be aware of the signs that they are running low emotionally, physically, and spiritually. We can only give what we have. Making sure caregivers are healthy and whole is paramount.

The better offer. We talked about moving away from the good-hearted "whatever you need, whenever you need it" offers. In reality, the majority of us do not mean "whatever-whenever" but have merely fallen into the habit of saying it. This puts the one who needs care at a profound disadvantage as they seek to understand exactly what each person means by "whatever" and "whenever." Caregivers can offer to care for someone with authenticity, intentionality, and forethought by framing their offer and answering the who, what, when, where, and why of it.

Caring cross-culturally. In our increasingly diverse world caring cross-culturally has become more important now than it ever has been. Seeking to understand the culture of the one we care for and our own culture will help caregivers provide more effective care. Our cultural backgrounds have a deep impact on how we care, and by being intentional in our pursuit of understanding, those we care for will feel valued and known.

Innovative culture of caring. Everett Rogers provides a model for those seeking to innovate their caring culture and provides a practical framework to begin diffusing the innovation. Innovating is not for the faint of heart and requires courage and determination. If innovators are persistent, they can progressively see incremental changes in culture as innovation is adopted.

What I believe is that if you and I can apply these basic principles which are found in this book, our world will be a more caring place. A place where people belong, matter, and are known. A world where people feel valued and where human dignity is once again at the forefront of our actions and deeds. A place where healing is taking place as we care for each other. What will your *caring life* look like and whose trajectory will you impact? I am excited to hear of the lives that will be changed because you have chosen to care.

Endnotes

1. Kucharski, A. (2020). *The Rules of Contagion: Why Things Spread—And Why They Stop*. Basic Books. 256.

2. Andrews, A. (2011). *The Noticer*. Thomas Nelson.

3. Campbell, R. (2018). *Radical Wisdom: A Daily Journal for Leaders*. iDisciple Publishing.

4. Brogden, D. (2022). *Proverbs: Amplified and Applied*. Abide Publishers.

5. Watson, J. (2008). *The Philosophy and Science of Caring*. University Press of Colorado. Ed. 1.

6. The Royal Rangers program is an activity-based, small group church ministry for boys and young men in grades K–12.

7. Maxwell, J. (2019). *Leadershift: 11 Essential Changes Every Leader Must Embrace*. HarperCollins Leadership. 2–3.

8. McHugh, A. S. (2015). *The Listening Life: Embracing Attentiveness in a World of Distraction*. IVP Books.

9. Cron, I. (2019). *Enneagram Made Simple*. Business Made Simple. USA. https://app.businessmadesimple.com/

c/3f38b1ca-8e49-48ec-97ba-3f59e120b28c, and DeGroat, C. (2020). *When Narcissism Comes to the Church: Healing Your Community From Emotional and Spiritual Abuse.* IVP.

10. Kahneman, D. Sibony, O., and Sunstein, C. (2021). *Noise: A Flaw in Human Judgment.* Little, Brown and Company. 31.

11. Chapman, G. (2014). *The Five Love Languages: The Secret to Love That Lasts.* Northfield Publishing.

12. There is a free assessment online to discover you love language (www.5lovelanguages.com/learn). I highly recommend it, if for nothing else than to learn more about yourself. It's a great place to start to explore how you want to be cared for and gives insight into how you may care for others.

13. Scazzero, P. (2017). *Emotionally Healthy Spirituality: It's Impossible to Be Spiritually Mature While Remaining Emotionally Immature.* Zondervan.

14. Campbell, R. (2018). *Radical Wisdom: A Daily Journal for Leaders.* iDisciple Publishing.

15. STL is an acronym for Speed the Light, a student-initiated, volunteer, charitable program that provides much-needed equipment to global workers across the United States and in over 180 countries around the world.

16. Cuss, S. (2019). *Managing Leadership Anxiety: Yours and Theirs.* Thomas Nelson.

17. Dodd, C. (2015). *Voice of the Heart: A Call to Full Living.* Sage Hill Publishing.

18. Foth, D. and Foth, R. (2017). *Known: Finding Deep Friendships in a Shallow World.* Waterbrook.

19. Kuest, R. (March 2022). "Ron Kuest on Conflict Management Techniques that Work." The Clarity Podcast.

20. Messner, M. (April 2020). "Mike Messner on Leadership Intelligence: Demonstrating the Characteristics of an Effective Leader." The Clarity Podcast.

21. Larson, E. (2020). *The Splendid and the Vile: A Saga of Churchill Family and Defiance During the Blitz.* Crown.

22. Patterson, K., Grenny, J., McMillan, R., & Switzler, A. (2002). *Crucial conversations.* McGraw-Hill Contemporary.

23. Toledo, A. 2019. *DNA of a Leader.* www.dnaofaleader.org.

24. Nieuwhof, C. (September 14, 2021). "Andy Stanley flips the mic to talk productivity secrets." The Carey Nieuwhof Leadership Podcast.

25. Nieuwhof, C. *9 Signs You Are Burning Out in Leadership.* https://careynieuwhof.com/9-signs-youre-burning-out-in-leadership/

26. Lingenfelter, S. (2008). *Leading Cross-Culturally: Covenant Relationships for Effective Christian Leadership.* Baker Academic.

27. Hofstede, G. (1991). *Cultures and Organizations : Software of the Mind.* McGraw-Hill.

28. Addington. T.J. (2014). *Deep Influence: Unseen Practices That Will Revolutionize Your Leadership.* Nav Press.

29. Rogers, E. (2003). *Diffusion of Innovations.* Free Press.

About the Author

Aaron Santmyire is a husband, father, nurse practitioner, podcast host, and most importantly a follower of Jesus. He is from the "almost heaven" state of West Virginia and has a Doctor of Nursing Practice from West Virginia University, an MBA from Southwestern Assemblies of God University (Texas), and a Bachelor of Arts in Bible and Missions from Southeastern University (Florida). Aaron has spent the last 20 years serving in Africa, specifically in Burkina Faso, Madagascar, and Kenya. He loves to trout fish, eat homemade apple pie, and cheer on the West Virginia Mountaineers.

Made in the USA
Coppell, TX
14 October 2022

84636631R00152